Praise for
The 7 Secrets of Responsive Leadership

"Jackie Jenkins-Scott is the kind of responsive, compassionate, and people-centered leader that our times demand and our communities deserve. I have had the joy and privilege of learning from her firsthand and I am so grateful that as we navigate turbulent times as a nation, she has put forth in writing her vision, insight, and approach. A must-read for those who want to lead with love and stay rooted in community."

> —AYANNA PRESSLEY, congresswoman from
> Massachusetts

"Jackie Jenkins-Scott provides a road map for effective leadership by laying bare the realities of the challenges, choices, and dilemmas that face leaders today. This is a must-read— a practical and thoughtful tool for anyone who aspires to become a responsive, effective, and successful leader."

> —DEBORAH C. JACKSON, president, Cambridge
> College

"*The 7 Secrets of Responsive Leadership* belongs on any leader's bookshelf, particularly one who understands the role of heart over head in motivating an organization. Jackie Jenkins-Scott has produced a highly readable, pragmatic, and emotionally intelligent book on a full range of leadership challenges and behaviors. The 7 Secrets are validated by multiple anecdotes from her own extensive leadership experience and peppered with real-world examples familiar to all of us."

> —BINK GARRISON, president of Bink, Inc.

"In *The 7 Secrets of Responsive Leadership,* Jackie skillfully helps leaders tackle complex leadership challenges with very practical and transparent advice. This is a unique and refreshing read for new and seasoned organizational leaders."

—DR. JOHN H. JACKSON, president and CEO of the Schott Foundation

"It was an honor to follow in the footsteps of Jackie's leadership at Dimock. The lessons in *The 7 Secrets of Responsive Leadership* remain a part of Dimock today and deeply resonate with me as they will for so many other leaders to come."

—MYECHIA MINTER-JORDAN, MD, MBA, former president and CEO, Dimock Center

"I've known Jackie for many years and she has always been a force of nature, enacting positive transformation within two of Boston's key health and educational institutions with her powerful brand of leadership. She has translated all of her experiences and knowledge about what it takes to be a truly effective leader into the pages that you hold before you, and I have no doubt that this, too, will be a tremendous success."

—STEVEN W. TOMPKINS, sheriff, Suffolk County, Massachusetts

The 7 SECRETS *of* RESPONSIVE LEADERSHIP

The 7 SECRETS *of* RESPONSIVE LEADERSHIP

Drive Change, Manage
Transitions, and Help Any
Organization Turn Around

JACKIE JENKINS-SCOTT

This edition first published in 2020 by Career Press, an imprint of
Red Wheel/Weiser, LLC

With offices at:
65 Parker Street, Suite 7
Newburyport, MA 01950
www.careerpress.com
www.redwheelweiser.com

ISBN: 978-1-63265-159-4

Library of Congress Cataloging-in-Publication Data available upon
request.

Cover design by Ellen Varitimos
Interior by Maureen Forys, Happenstance Type-O-Rama
Typeset in New Baskerville and Trade Gothic

Printed in the United States of America
IBI

10 9 8 7 6 5 4 3 2 1

With Love and Gratitude

To my large extended family—past and present—who provide a foundation of unconditional love and encouragement

To my amazing sister-friends who lift and support me through the good times and the challenging times

To all the emerging responsive leaders who aim to make the world a more just and humane place for all

To Amal and Amber, who make me proud each and every day

And to Jim, who has been by my side through it all.

Acknowledgments

The process of preparing and writing this book reminded me that we do not lead alone and that I am no exception to this. Countless unnamed people contributed to my journey of learning and growing as a leader. With gratitude and appreciation, I thank them all.

For twenty-one years, I had the great privilege of leading the Dimock Community Health Center (now called The Dimock Center). I will always be grateful to the dedicated and committed members of the board of directors who guided and supported me as a young emerging leader. In particular, I am thankful for the excellent board leaders, Walter Jennings, Joseph Feaster, Wendell Knox, and Clayton Turnbull, who each served as board chair for a time during my tenure as president.

The compassionate and dedicated Dimock staff who provided care to the patients and clients we served were truly an inspiration. In particular, I thank Dr. Herb Dreyer for his commitment to our patients, day and night. He and I were privileged to work alongside amazing caregivers during the early days of the AIDS pandemic. I thank the patients and our caregivers who taught us so much about living and dying with compassion and dignity.

The Dimock story is a story of vision, leadership, and legacy. I am grateful for the many supporters—philanthropic and community—who believe in this institution. I especially acknowledge the late William O. Taylor, publisher of the *Boston Globe*, who was one of our very early supporters and the first to make a $500,000 investment in Dimock. With gratitude, I thank the many donors who followed his lead in ensuring that this great community resource continues to serve those in need.

Today, Dimock is thriving and provides services to thousands of people. With great appreciation, I thank all who have continued Dimock's mission and legacy with professionalism and dedication as a true testament to the power of resilience.

I acknowledge with gratitude Robert Lincoln, who, as chair of the board of Wheelock College, took a risk in hiring a nontraditional president and who supported me for the twelve years I served in that role. I thank the remarkable Wheelock alumni who welcomed me with open arms and supported our many efforts to continue Wheelock's important mission.

During my presidency, I learned so much from Wheelock students who, with their optimism, curiosity, and desire to make the world better, always provided the boost I needed to keep going. I thank my colleague and friend Marta Rosa, who assisted in recalling the Mattahunt story, for her support during very challenging times. I want to especially acknowledge Sister Janet Eisner, president of Emmanuel College, who supported and encouraged me as a new college president and who continues to serve as a role model for what it means to successfully lead in an ever-changing higher education environment.

I have been most fortunate to work with many truly gifted servant leaders during my career. I am grateful for each of them who trusted me and who I trusted to lead with integrity, passion, and a dedication to excellence. I will be forever grateful for all that we were able to accomplish together.

For over twenty years, Valerie Thornhill Hudson worked by my side supporting me and the institutions I led. Thank you Val, for keeping me on track and helping me shine in so many, many ways!

A special thank you to all those who encouraged me to write this book and helped bring it to fruition. Maryann Karinch, for your encouragement, terrific advice, thorough research, and excellent ideas. Thanks also to my supportive team at Red Wheel/Weiser, especially my editor Michael Pye, marketing champion Laurie Kelly-Pye, and the production team, especially Jane Hagaman, Maureen Forys, and Rebecca Rider.

To all the special women in my life—thank you! You have lifted me and supported me in so many ways. I have relied on your wise counsel, love, and support through thick and thin.

Finally, I offer my love and appreciation to my family. Those who paved the way for me to become the woman I am—my grandparents, parents, and many aunts, uncles, cousins, and other relatives. My children, Amal and Amber, give me the gift of unconditional love, and I continue to learn from them each day. And Jim, my life partner, love, and friend, you have walked this path with me, and I couldn't ask for a more loving and committed partner. Thank you!

Contents

Introduction:

The Nature of Responsive Leadership

Leaders who pride themselves on being turnaround experts put the goal of radical change upfront and seek opportunities to fulfill that goal. Similarly, leaders with a burning desire to make the world a better place put *that* mission upfront and look for venues in which to fulfill it.

Some of these leaders are highly accomplished and valuable, but they rely on what I call *systematic leadership.* They carry a set of methods and laws—principles governing actions—with them everywhere they go. Generally, they are hired because they are competent in applying those methods and laws in different places. They have the ability, intention, and focus to get organizations to respond *to them* and to their style of leading. In the extreme, these systematic leaders are the type President Dwight D. Eisenhower criticized when he said, "You do not lead by hitting people over the head—that's assault, not leadership."

I'm more of a "surprise me!" kind of person. I invite the universe to pique my curiosity, show me new ways to learn, and invite me into new leadership challenges by helping me recognize opportunities. For these reasons, I describe what I offer you as *responsive leadership*.

In moving through life, I look for opportunities. Goals, missions, and strategies come out of seizing these. For example, I saw the opportunity to lead a struggling college; then the requirements of leadership took shape: the goal of turning it around, the mission of giving students unprecedented chances for growth, and the strategies to support the goal and mission.

Responsive leaders are very focused on the people—*the humanity*—within the opportunity. For example, I joined the Wheelock College community because I believed it had the potential to improve the lives of children and families. I came to Wheelock because I believe deeply in higher education and its power to lift people out of poverty to places where they can change communities and society as a whole for the better. Yes, in a strictly business sense, the opportunity was to effect a turnaround. However, it would have meant very little to me to succeed if I didn't see what that meant in terms of people's lives. I need to be in a position from which I can make systemic change, where I can work on challenges that are transformational.

When people interview someone for the senior executive position at an organization, they always ask, "What's your vision for the job?" A systematic leader can pull that answer out of his pocket; he comes in with a clear idea of what he can do and what he wants to do. If you're a responsive leader, however, you think, "How the hell am I supposed to know that? I'm interviewing for the job and won't know until I'm on the job."

A characteristic of a responsive leader is her desire for a shared vision. It's not about imposing what one person thinks should happen on others, it's about responding to the genuine needs of the organization and building a vision shared by the people who aim to meet those needs. You are never just responding, however. Every step of the way, you are leading by example so that people *respond to you* in a way that shapes the culture of your organization. If you want people to work hard, you must work hard. If you want people to be transparent, then you have to be transparent. If you want honesty to be a pervasive trait of your organization, then you must be honest. If you want people to treat each other with fairness, then you must be fair.

Okay, now let's introduce the formula for responsive leadership. When you blend flour, baking powder, salt, and a little milk, you get batter. As any cook knows, you can do a million things with that batter.

This is a metaphor for responsive leadership. A little of this and a little of that, or lots of this and less of that, depending on the circumstances. Then you blend and you put your metaphorical batter to work in myriad environments. This style of leadership proves versatile and transferrable. And like the recipe for a basic batter, it's relatively easy to teach.

Implementing responsive leadership begins with how you treat yourself and interact with the people closest to you.

I am a very driven person when it comes to work ethics and established objectives. Generally, I wake up with a clear idea of what I need to do. At that moment, my mission is to focus, organize, motivate, and energize myself. In other words, I begin every day by trying to lead myself. I am responsive to myself.

This may help explain why I stay in jobs and relationships so long. Every day is going somewhere—*I'm* going somewhere—and that is an exciting prospect. It's one that sustains my enthusiasm for my work, family, friends, and volunteer activities.

Now, let's look at this situation from a different perspective. Perhaps it's *because* I have long-term relationships at the core of my life that I have the ability to serve as a leader in different environments and industries. And then building on that experience, I am in a position to go to the next level—to teach others how to cultivate leadership. In my heart, I think that's what I was born to do.

That is the impetus behind this book.

Psychologist Abraham Maslow introduced his theory on the hierarchy of needs in a 1943 paper called "A Theory of Human Motivation." He postulated that, unless the lower human needs related to survival and security are met, a person lacks the psychological juice to pursue "growth needs." The floor of the pyramid of needs is made up of biological imperatives such as food, sleep, and air. Just above that are requirements for safety and security. Above that, interactions between people enter into the hierarchy. Therefore, the third floor up is about needing to belong and to love and be loved. It covers the human need for affection, relationships, camaraderie.

What's after that? The growth needs—the tier of esteem needs such as a sense of achievement and reputation. And then, at the top, is self-actualization, which is what any leader hopes to achieve. At that peak part of the pyramid, the focus is on the need to solve problems and live a life infused with morality and creativity. Celebrities like Leonardo DiCaprio, an environmental activist, and Oprah Winfrey, arguably one of the most potent forces for positive action today, live in the realm of self-actualization. Corporate leaders like Richard Branson seem to live in this realm as well. I've also known teachers, mothers, and preachers to live in this place.

Without giving Maslow full credit for understanding what drives people, we can certainly give him a generous amount. If you are part of a group that is starving to death, for instance, you might have the leadership ability to pull your group together to find food, but if you do not find food, how long will your reign as leader last? The same is true with safety. When a population is ravaged by war and is focused on day-to-day survival, people are looking for a safe haven. If you can provide it for a while, you surface as a leader, but you are ousted if you cannot restore safety in the long term. When those physiological and safety needs are met, the life-blood of your existence becomes your human (and other animal) connections.

Those connections are a source of emotional and cognitive feedback; they give you the sustenance to mature as a human being—in short, as long as they are in place, you have what it takes to be a responsive leader.

Practically speaking, let's explore how the connections serve you as you change roles and environments throughout your career. For me, each turn in the path of my career did not mean easing around a curve and then gunning the gas to go full speed ahead. I came to a full stop and then took two complementary actions:

1. I performed a heart check. I asked myself, "What about this next activity gives me an emotional connection to it?" Talking with people in my inner circle was always a good way to identify why, and how, I felt drawn to an opportunity.

2. I made a calculation about the direction I thought I should take. For example, before going into

coaching and consulting full-time, I wanted to illuminate my path by learning what the best coaches and consultants had to offer. Cultivating leadership involves learning. You might be genetically gifted in many ways, but without cultivating the skills and absorbing the wisdom of people who are proven leaders—as well as listening to trusted advisors—you cheat yourself. You don't know everything, no matter how much confidence in your abilities you have. You need to know what the leaders who have gone before you know. History, and the stars of history, are great teachers. And you need to know what the people you trust have to say to you.

You make an intention to be great. And then you work at it. An integral part of your success is that you have as a constant those connections in your life that keep you on track morally, creatively, and cognitively.

Do you want to be a responsive leader? The first, and critical, step is valuing and enriching your connections with family, friends, and colleagues whom you trust.

1

Secret 1—
Take Advantage of Opportunity

During a conference of corporate directors, a few of us discussed the attributes of leadership over dinner. The conversation became a collection of bits we had read, heard from speakers, and lived. Ultimately, we agreed that the strongest leaders have these characteristics, which we dubbed the *Big 4:*

Curiosity: A desire to continuously learn, discover, and grow intellectually

Humility: A sincere regard for the reality that we cannot go it alone

Empathy: The ability to feel and appreciate other human beings

Resilience: The capacity to recover, to keep going forward in the face of adversity

Note that we agreed these were qualities of the *strongest* leaders—not necessarily the most famous, richest, or most powerful. Throughout this book, I will try to channel the wisdom of these women and men so you can be reminded of how critical the Big 4 are in making the 7 Secrets of responsive leadership come alive for you.

I rediscovered the Big 4 in my journal after I had already drafted descriptions of the 7 Secrets. As I went through the how-to information and stories for my proposed book, I realized that each of the four surfaced in each of the secrets! It was like finding the magic ingredients in soil that allowed amazing flowers, vegetables, and trees to grow. I think we can all easily agree that curiosity plays a central role in discovering opportunity, for example. At the same time, considering the other three—who, other than you, is integral to the opportunity (humility), who these people are in terms of their values and priorities (empathy), and how well you are likely to adapt within that opportunity (resilience)—is vitally important in deciding whether an opportunity is a good one for you.

Do a Google search on the discrete phrase "characteristics of leadership," and the result is roughly nine million entries that offer the top five, top ten, and so on, traits of a leader. Many appear to be results-oriented such as *innovation*. I'm not sure how important it is for a leader to be innovative if she is curious and humble enough to hire innovative people. Other lists talk about *passion*. To me, passion is a personal driver. I have passion for what I do, but I think it varies from day to day as to how much that internal fire contributes to my ability to lead. As I probed and read entries on the internet, I felt reinforced that the short list our dinner group composed might be the best of all.

The Institute of Leadership and Management lists the following Five Dimensions of Leadership: achievement, authenticity, collaboration, ownership, and vision. You could make the case that the Big 4 make it more likely that a person could capture the Institute's Five Dimensions. It all depends on how each of the dimensions is interpreted; that is, whether the emphasis is on quantitative criteria or qualitative. To differentiate, if you evaluate a leader based on quarterly returns and name-recognition, that's a *quantitative* analysis of achievement. If you evaluate based on processes installed and people hired to support the organization's success, that is more of a *qualitative* focus.

Quantitative measures address results of leadership that come and go. In fact, we might say that they relate more to management—the technical aspects of leadership—rather than leadership traits. They do not describe the sustained attributes that make a person's leadership strong in both triumph and crisis as well as transportable and transferrable to different environments.

EXPLORING THE BIG 4 IN LEADERS

With a laser focus on the Big 4, let's look at how they have surfaced, or failed to surface, in several leaders. Not all are household names, but you'll find the work they've done familiar.

Patricia Moore

Patricia Moore (author of *Disguised*) was originally drawn to art but later migrated into a career in industrial design. Sister Mary Ellen Twist, president of Mt. Mercy Academy and one of her early teachers, described her as

> . . . *inquisitive, [driven] to ask a lot of questions . . .*
> *I think it is true that Patty's early education had something*

to do with her attitude and her values, and especially her respect for all people.[1]

In 1974 when she began her foray into her chosen field, Moore was the only female in a design group of 350 people working with Raymond Loewy, considered the Father of Industrial Design. As such, she described her voice as uncommon among the others in the room. Her constant "What about . . . ?" questions related to people with mobility issues such as paraplegics and people with severe arthritis would elicit the response, "Patty, we don't design for *those* people."

A few years later—at the age of twenty-six—Moore embarked on what is known as *experiential empathy*. She worked with others to develop the protheses and makeup she needed to age her appearance to around eighty and added glasses with clouded lenses so she could experience the diminished vision of many elderly people. She also blunted her hearing, strapped splints to her legs to impose movement restrictions, and wore gloves to reduce her dexterity. After all this effort, she could no longer function as a young person. As she traveled throughout the United States and Canada over the next three years, she became dependent on the assistance of total strangers she met on the streets.

In 1980, Moore founded her first company to develop new products and services for the cradle-to-grave needs of people of all abilities. It evolved into her current company, MooreDesign Associates, where she serves as president. Her clients include some of the biggest companies in the world.

Whether you describe what Moore did as recognizing an opportunity or creating one, she launched her business by defining a need that she had the ability to meet.

It's analogous to Henry Ford realizing that average people, not just rich people, could and should benefit from having automobiles; he then mass-produced the Model T. He and Moore both revolutionized economic and social possibilities for significant populations.

R. Roger Remington, Massimo and Lella Vignelli Distinguished Professor of Design, honored what we would see as the vision behind Patricia Moore's leadership, noting:

> *She identified early in her career a need and a problem and she structured a definite response to that need and I think we're all very proud of that accomplishment and I think it's something that really sticks out as a recognizable benchmark in her career.*[2]

Moore's persistent goal, then, was to design "with equity." She addressed myriad basic problems of dexterity and comfort, such as the thick-handled, rubber-grip kitchen appliances that became OXO Good Grips. She successfully challenged people who refused to finance her mammography project—a quick-release mechanism that would immediately stop exerting pressure on a breast after the image was taken. Essentially, her style of leadership brought others toward empathy and away from their natural tendency to be insensitive and obsessed with the bottom line.

> *Moore's philosophy is that design should empower people and not disable them: "Each of us has some level of capacity, some level of ability. Design is intended to meet that level and exceed it. . . . Whenever there's a roadblock in our lives, it's because somebody didn't do their job right."*[3]

Moore captures all four attributes of leadership, with curiosity and empathy abundantly obvious. She also exhibits humility with her respect for the knowledge that people with mobility difficulties have about their own needs. She has stepped back to listen and observe repeatedly to complement her own experience, rather than simply having it dominate her choices. Moore's resilience is apparent in her struggles against powerful voices who didn't see the economic sense in her desire to serve all people through design, not just fully functioning ones.

Howard Schultz

Well known as the former Starbucks Corporation Chairman, in 2018 Howard Schultz (*Onward: How Starbucks Fought for Its Life without Losing Its Soul*) reminded the world that the management of his company had a moral compass. After two black men were arrested at a Philadelphia store because they used the restroom before they purchased anything, Schultz stepped into the spotlight and condemned the action the Starbucks manager had taken. He pledged to address an obvious problem of unconscious bias. He did not back off from the bitter words *racial profiling* in saying that the company would make racial bias training mandatory for every one of its 175,000 employees.

Schultz did not have a sudden flash of conscience or empathy: what he did was consistent with how he had lead the company for many years. It seemed as though he never forgot his roots—the Bay View Houses housing project in southeastern Brooklyn—and wanted to create opportunities and rewards for others who worked hard to get an education and succeed. He wanted to shape an organization that practiced empathy for staff (who he called *partners*) and customers alike. One of his groundbreaking initiatives that gave fuel to that empathy was the Starbucks College

Achievement Plan, developed in alliance with Arizona State University (ASU) President Michael Crow. Through it, partners could pursue their college education tuition-free using ASU's online resources.

Schultz's curiosity score was high in that he relentlessly sought ways to build the company, ultimately helping it deliver approximately 18,000 percent in shareholder returns since its initial public offering in 1992.[4] Humility shone through in the way he put the team's input upfront when he was deciding how to grow the company and determining what the mechanisms were for turning a profit. Without question, the way he treated people—and not just when the company's reputation was under threat—indicated a consistent desire to honor their dignity. Resilience was threaded through his entire career with the company—from coming on as director of retail operation for a company selling coffee beans (not coffee), to taking an eight-year hiatus as senior leader, to returning in 2008 to restore the company's reputation and profits after they faltered.

Colin Powell

The former US Secretary of State called his 2003 speech justifying the war in Iraq a blot on his record.[5] Without a doubt, Colin Powell's (*My American Journey*) leadership embodied the Big 4, yet the "blot" is a valuable lesson that even great leaders can make great mistakes when one or two of the Big 4 get submerged by powerful influences.

Powell grew up in Harlem, the son of Jamaican immigrants, and he attended New York City public schools. At City College of New York (CCNY), he found his calling and joined the Reserve Officers' Training Corps (ROTC), and thus his military career was launched. The Big 4 shone through time and again, with Powell earning eleven military decorations in his career—he was curious about solutions, resilient during the stresses of war, team-oriented, and focused on the needs of fellow soldiers. He earned one award for rescuing comrades from a burning helicopter after he, too, was injured in the crash. And in September 2006, he joined like-minded Senate Republicans in supporting more rights and better treatment for detainees at the Guantanamo Bay detention facility in Cuba.[6]

Where Colin Powell failed—how he got his blot—suggests that he did not remain curious or humble enough to counter the force of a US president directing him to go the United Nations and make the case for war against Iraq. Asking more questions about evidence of weapons of mass destruction, relying more on people in the field who were trusted sources—these are just two of the measures Powell might have taken to display great leadership in that situation. He later explained that language and "facts" had not even come from President Bush, who sent him to the UN, but rather from Vice President Dick Cheney:

> I'm secretary of state. Who else would you send? You can't send the secretary of defense to the U.N. The U.N. ambassador—this is a little above that pay grade. So he selected me, and I think he thought I had credibility to deliver a speech, and it would be believable.

> The speech supposedly had been prepared in the White House in the NSC [National Security Council]. But when we were given what had been prepared, it was totally inadequate, and we couldn't track anything in it. When I asked Condi Rice, the national security advisor, where did this come from, it turns out the vice president's office had written it.[7]

In hindsight, Powell realized that he had strayed from the principles that had guided him so well. He did what many great leaders have done throughout history: allowed powerful influences to corrupt his judgment and behavior.

TAKING ADVANTAGE OF OPPORTUNITY

With these profiles in mind, consider the primary focus of this chapter: taking advantage of opportunity. Now ask yourself this question: *Why* would you want to take advantage of an opportunity? Is it because you see the possibility for acclaim, fame, power, and possibly wealth? Or is it because you have what it takes internally to make this a radiant opportunity for a team, an organization?

This chapter explores how to take advantage of opportunity when you see success within yourself, within others, and within the combination of forces that is your organization.

At its core, this book is about the intimate relationship between leadership and opportunity, so this opening chapter is primarily about identifying and timing opportunity:

- What constitutes a good opportunity? In other words, how do you detect the signs that success for you, and for others around you, is probable?

- When is a desirable time to take advantage of a good opportunity?

My Story: Seeing Past the Ruins

First, let me introduce you to my story of stepping into my first major role as a leader; it sets the stage for a close look at the steps for identifying a good opportunity. Naturally, much insight into spotting an opportunity came to me in retrospect. At the time I plunged into the senior executive role at The Dimock Community Health Center (now The Dimock Center), I was still green, but I was sure of one thing: the people at this place emanated and demonstrated a commitment to their work that gave me a positive feeling about our future together.

My story begins in my early thirties, when I worked on Michael Dukakis's second campaign for Governor of Massachusetts. When the election was over, I had the option of going to work for him, but around the same time, an acquaintance told me about a top position at a community health organization that was in trouble.

I resisted hearing what my acquaintance had to say, because going to work for a political leader I admired held great appeal at this time. I would have proximity to power, a responsibility to the people of my state, and would play a role in upgrading our government—all of this kept luring me toward the State House in Boston.

However, this acquaintance, who worked at the health center, was relentless. "Just talk to them," he begged. He argued that a facility serving the families of a largely African-American community should have at least one applicant of color.

I had seen Dimock before but felt no particular connection. Learning a little about the organization from this acquaintance aroused my curiosity, though, and I started to learn more. And I did end up applying for the job of president and chief executive officer.

As part of the interview process, I was given a tour of the campus. During it, I felt as though I'd come home, that this was where I belonged. That was the romantic part of the experience.

The reality I also absorbed involved dilapidated buildings, depressed employees, and financial devastation. Although it sat on ten acres of desirable real estate in Boston, Dimock was in receivership—it was not looking good from a business perspective for any reason other than its land.

And yet, despite its challenges, the staff at Dimock made every effort to help the people of nearby neighborhoods. They cared about their patients, most of whom had very limited means, and their hospital. Their depression was superseded by their commitment to stick to their standards and serve their community. When I saw that, I knew that this was where I belonged, not in state government.

A twenty-one-year experience of responsive leadership began at that moment on my tour.

Dimock is in an inner-city Boston neighborhood called Roxbury, which lays claim to being "the heart of black culture in Boston."[8] Polish immigrants, led by Dr. Marie Zakrzewska, founded it in 1862 as the New England Hospital for Women and Children. The July it opened, it had ten beds housed in a small wooden building on Pleasant Street in Roxbury. At the time, it was the only hospital in New England opened by and operated by women with a mission to serve women, and it was only the second such hospital in the country. It rose to be recognized as a facility of great distinction and covered the entire range of women-related services in a single institution: medical, surgical, obstetrical, and pediatric. Dimock was also the first hospital in the country to establish a school for nurses. America's first trained nurse, Linda Richards, graduated in 1873. Mary Eliza Mahoney, the country's first black nurse, graduated in 1879.

The most immediate opportunity for me was to help Dimock survive—that is, to dig it out from financial ruin. But I saw another one peeking through the dark clouds of bankruptcy: the opportunity to restore Dimock to greatness—to honor its rich history of service by bringing more buildings and programs to life.

Steps to Identifying a Good Opportunity

Now that you know a bit about my first opportunity, you'd probably like to know how to identify one for yourself. Your steps to identifying an opportunity worth pursuing are guided by five key interrogatives: why, who, what, where, and how. The questions that help you step toward or away from an opportunity line up like this:

- Why me?

- Who else?

- What went wrong/right?

- Where did the organization come from?

- Where could it go?

- How excited am I?

Why Me?

An opportunity has the potential to be labeled good if you're well-suited for it. For many people—me included—this starts when you perceive a need that you believe you can address and feel compelled to do so. That is clearly where Patricia Moore started in her industrial design business.

Most people are not as clear-headed as Moore, how-ever; it takes some time to find genuinely good oppor-tunities. Think about the jobs you sought or accepted before you had a sense of your own self-worth and skills. Maybe you were lucky and went straight from playing video games to designing video games, but most peo-ple take a snakier path to their career. The average per-son changes jobs ten to fifteen times during his or her career.[9] One of the millennials I interviewed for this book had already held six full-time, career-related jobs in the ten years since she had graduated from college.

When my acquaintance told me about the position at Dimock, I questioned his logic. One thing was for sure: I did not want the answer to "Why me?" to be simply "Because of the color of your skin." At the same time, his reasoning in linking my skin color to the relevance of applying for the job did make sense.

There was a deeper answer to the question, however. In reviewing my own catalog of credentials, I considered that I had a master's degree in social work, previous busi-ness experience at an executive level, and the kind of agility in problem-solving that comes with working on a political campaign.

My collection of answers to "Why me?" indicated that this was an opportunity for which I was well-matched. That's one small step toward it, but without knowing more about the people, history, and facilities of the cen-ter, I couldn't yet ascertain whether or not this was an opportunity worth seizing. I'll spend more time on those factors in the upcoming subsections.

One of my friends heard about a huge opportunity just a little over a year after she got her master's degree in theater arts. Right after graduating, she taught the summer semester of a theater program, then got a job as an office manager in an investment banking firm. She had to pay some grad school bills and teaching was not going to cover that expense, so she relied on her office skills. One day, an investment analyst at the firm told her about a job at a theater she liked to attend: managing director. Her heart raced until she said to herself: "Why me? All I have is a master's degree in theater arts, not business. How could I manage a professional theater?"

Her boss, the owner of the company, gave her the insight she needed to compose a better answer. He reminded her that

- She managed an office, serving high-dollar, demanding clients and a senior staff of Ivy League financial pros.

- Within three months, she had revamped internal systems to cut costs and boost efficiency.

- He regularly sought her input on prospectuses because of the quality of her writing.

- She managed three classes of teenagers at her teaching job and he figured if she could do that, she could run the country, not just a theater.

My friend put that together with her "measly" master's degree and a few other work experiences and realized she had a darned good answer to "Why me?" She sought the position and got it.

Each time you face an opening that seems desirable, ask yourself that self-reflection question and then give yourself time to answer it. Just like how I faced the Dimock opportunity and my friend considered whether to pursue the theater management position, all the answers don't necessarily pop into your head immediately.

The way of organizing your thoughts that I recommend comes from *Control the Conversation,* a book primarily about how to respond well to questions. One of the authors, James O. Pyle, developed the program that teaches US military interrogators questioning skills during their training in SERE (Survival, Evasion, Resistance, and Escape) school. Pyle sorts areas of both discovery (questioning) and disclosure (answering questions) into these four: people, places, things, and time. These are the four organizing principles we'll use throughout this section on the questions that help you take steps toward, or away from, an opportunity.

Let's start with my Dimock opportunity. Why me?

People: I'm a qualified African-American eyeing an opportunity to run an organization primarily serving people of color.

Places: The position is in a city I know well—my home city of Boston. Also, the facilities themselves have allure for me. As run-down as they were, their historical significance and basic aesthetics invited my appreciation.

Things: An appropriate graduate degree and work experience that cultivated vital skills gave a good credentials-based answer to the question.

Time: I was about to make a change anyway!

Who Else?

Not only do you need to know who you will lead, but also to whom you will report—you will be leading them, too, by the way—and who will view you as an equal.

This is a people question, but to answer it well, consider what those people do, where they do it, how time-sensitive their work is, and so on, as you answer the question.

As I mentioned in my story, the staff at Dimock rose above depressing working conditions and relentless demands to serve the people in nearby neighborhoods. They cared about their patients and the quality of their care—knowing full well that Dimock would not receive appropriate compensation for most medical services. When I saw their work and met some of them, I knew the most important answer to "Who else?" It was "decent, dedicated people, who try not to delay in providing care." The board of trustees that stuck by them shared their values and work ethic. And then, there was the neighborhood: it needed Dimock and Dimock was born to serve that need.

But this isn't just a book for do-gooders in the traditional nonprofit sense. The question of "who else?" applies to every leader in every environment. One of the people interviewed for this book refused what was, ostensibly, a great opportunity to lead one division of a law enforcement operation. He thought the team reporting to him comprised outstanding officers, but the main person responsible for oversight of the operation made comments in the interview that suggested she was ethically challenged.

Another contributor took a job offer because the salary was three times what she had been making. She had a unique expertise that this employer needed, so it was not unjustified. In addition to the salary, she assumed the prestigious title of vice president of marketing. Within a few months, however, she suspected that the company's programmers had stolen code from a previous employer, that the CEO doctored financials given to investors, and that the company lawyer had just taken the big salary to put her kids through private school.

In other words, she had not made "Who else?" a priority question in stepping toward the opportunity.

What Went Wrong? What Went Right?

At Dimock, signs of financial devastation were everywhere. But as my friend who took over the professional theater discovered, with a quick look at the summary financials, I found that the deficits were something that had worsened over time. The cascading effect of poor decisions and misguided investments had brought each institution into a financial crisis state. Neither of the answers to "What went wrong?" for these businesses could be as well-defined as catastrophic moments in corporate history like the introduction of New Coke, which lasted on the market for seventy-nine days, or Excite (now Ask .com), which decided not to purchase Google for a paltry $750,000. (Its total net worth is now more than $7 trillion).

Leaders who like a turn-around challenge can be drawn to scrutinize "What went wrong?" more than any other aspect of the opportunity. If you're one of them, you find satisfaction in knowing that something *did* go wrong, and you want to fix it even before you hang your pictures on the office wall. This one question could be the most compelling for you, submerging you in some of the self-reflection or team issues that are vital in making a sound decision on your next step.

But throttle back: these questions are not a system of weighted variables. Each guides you in the steps you take toward or away from an opportunity. Give each one the importance it is due.

You also need to immediately start exploring the companion question: What went right?

At Dimock, the biggest thing that went right was that services to the community continued and board members did what they knew how to do to support the staff in their efforts. That was a huge right. It made Dimock seem healthy at its core. For me, it made the wrong of financial disaster seem like a curable infection.

Where Did the Organization Come From?

Dimock set precedent after precedent in the healthcare field from the time it opened in 1862. It stood alone in the region as being operated by women with a mission to serve women; only one other hospital in the country was anything like it. It also had the first hospital-based school for nurses, graduating America's first formally trained nurse as well as the country's first black nurse.

Such a rich history might inspire a leader to envision either a systematic return to past glory or, while cherishing it, a radical departure from the past. But the insight as to whether the opportunity to lead the organization is a good one should not be centered on that personal vision. "Where did the organization come from?" should not be a question that evokes answers focused on externals alone. In Dimock's case, this would mean conjuring up an image of a beautiful Victorian building, staff basking in national renown, and sufficient operating funds.

The answer to the question must include the essence of the organization—its life force, its mission. In Dimock's case, this is a desire to "heal and uplift individuals, families, and community."

Where did Apple come from? Not from engineering specifications and an almost cult-like following, but from Steve Jobs' intent "to make a contribution to the world by making tools for the mind that advance humankind."[10]

Of course, organizational mission statements can evolve, but a leader might want to rethink whether an opportunity is "good" if none of the original DNA is left—or if he thinks that the only way to save the place is to make that kind of change. In the case of my position with Dimock, such an approach would have meant that I came in as CEO and initiated the process of tearing down the hospital and building condos.

Where Could It Go?

Before you answer this question, you want to have clarity on two things:

1. Whether the organization, composed of its governing body, staff, and constituents, is open to having it go *anywhere.*

   The gutters of Wall Street are littered with companies that lost value because a founder or board of directors rebuffed the wisdom and skill of the leader who wanted to implement change. These executives eyed the opportunity to make a difference and yet seemed to overestimate the openness that the power structure had to organizational change. As a result, we saw companies like Best Buy being kicked aside by Amazon, for example.

2. Where it's going now—before you get there.

   An organization can be going one of three ways, or it can be going all of three ways. You might eye an opportunity and conclude the company is headed toward the summit, sliding downhill, or rolling along a plateau. Look more closely—stay curious—and you might notice something very different. Perhaps its products have superior quality, but profits are declining, and its reputation and customer service are in a state of status quo. It's going three directions at once.

When I considered the chief leadership role at Dimock, I saw an organization maintaining services on a fairly even level, financially plunging into the abyss, and facilities and a reputation that were degrading over time.

Once you've made the assessment of where the organization is going without you, then move on to thinking about where it could go *with* you. Where it's excelling, or at least doing fine, do you have a sense of what talent and other human, as well as material, resources will help improve performance? Similarly, with the aspects of the organization in stasis or decline, do you feel prepared to get momentum going, or are you clueless, yet hopeful, about fixing problems? You want to feel your resilience rising inside you as you recognize shortcomings of the organizations. You want to feel your curiosity going into overdrive.

If you and the opportunity are a great match, it's the answer to this question that sends you to the final question and the final step in your decision-making.

How Excited Am I?

The other interrogatives guided you through vital mental processes. Now it's time to get physical.

What does your gut tell you about the opportunity? You will have an emotional response to it that lets your heart help guide you in deciding whether or not you should take on this particular leadership role. When I walked across the Dimock campus for the first time, I felt I'd come home. It was a full-bodied feeling of positive energy.

The relevance of a feeling like that to serving as a leader within an organization is the essence of Chapter 2.

GAUGING THE TIMING

Opportunities can be like the weather in Rapid City, South Dakota, which has the most unpredictable weather in the United States according to *National Geographic.*

First, an opportunity might hit you without warning. After you observe it briefly and find it interesting, you can collect what you believe to be relevant data so you understand the phenomenon and try to answer basic questions: Why did this occur now? What's the significance of my going into the middle of this right now?

One skill a responsive leader must have is being able to ascertain the best possible moment at which to seize an opportunity. It's a Goldilocks issue: the porridge can't be too hot or too cold.

The friend I referenced earlier who took the position as managing director of a professional theater told me a fun story about timing. The theater had a season of hit plays and she felt they might have missed revenue opportunities by not having a larger space. If they had the same good fortune the following season, she thought they should be prepared to move a hit show to a bigger theater.

She scored a meeting with a famous Broadway producer and asked him, "How will I know when it's time to move to a larger space?" He smiled and leaned toward her: "When the line for tickets wraps around the block."

The lesson? The ideal time to take advantage of an opportunity is when it's obvious it is the right time.

One of the contributors to this book declined a position on the faculty of a local college. As a recently retired, award-winning journalist, she was well-suited for teaching her craft, and this opportunity would have given her a lead role in reshaping the journalism curriculum. But the timing was off and she knew it: she was using her newfound free hours to get up to speed on the many flavors of online journalism, but she wasn't there yet. The position would have been great for her, but she felt it wouldn't have been so good for the students who might get an overabundance of old-school thinking.

The lesson here builds on the first one. The conditions were not present for the retired journalist to successfully execute the mission. In this case, it was a matter of her not being ready, but in many cases, it is the organization that is not ready for the leader.

In leaving behind a potential job at the Massachusetts State House and choosing to pursue the senior executive position at Dimock, I felt as certain as the producer seeing the line for tickets wrap around the block. The voice inside me said, "Don't hesitate. Time to move."

In addition to major, career-changing opportunities that come along, once you are in a position of leadership, you need the same skills of identification and timing to determine how to pick your priorities. More on that in the upcoming chapters.

2

Secret 2—
Compete Well by
Leading with Heart

I t takes more than knowledge and guts to lead in troubling times. It takes heart.

Some leaders are driven by their intellect and some are driven by their heart. Ideally, leaders bring both to the job, but knowing which part of you is more likely to chart your path is critical. Keep in mind that great leaders guided by their hearts do not leave their brains behind and just do what feels right. Mother Theresa founded a religious order of more than 4,500 sisters who were active in 133 countries. It takes intelligence and planning to do heart work effectively.

Leading with heart is a natural outgrowth of having two of the Big 4: empathy and humility. In turn, leading with heart reinforces these strengths.

Now let's add a tool that brings empathy and humility together with curiosity and resilience in a corporate environment: *vulnerability.*

Understanding vulnerability as a tool of leadership is a good way to move closer toward leading with heart.

Professor Brené Brown (*Daring Greatly*) is well known for her research into the nature and benefits of vulnerability. After years of study and thousands of interviews, she concluded that the core of vulnerability is courage, specifically the courage to be imperfect. Note well: *courage* has its origins in the Latin word *cor,* or heart.

In 2010, Brown gave a TEDx talk called "The Power of Vulnerability" that scored millions of views over the following weeks. Fortune 500 companies were among the many groups, large and small, that invited her to speak. Oddly, many of the corporate executives who contacted her asked her *not* to talk about vulnerability and, instead, focus on innovation, creativity, and change. In a 2012 follow-up presentation she gave on the TED mainstage, Brown told the audience what she told the executives: "Vulnerability is the birthplace of innovation, creativity and change. To create is to make something that has never existed before. There's nothing more vulnerable than that. Adaptability to change is all about vulnerability."[1]

In short, vulnerability gives you the strength to invest in relationships, even when you're not sure they will work out. Whether you're a leader or not, hopefully that investment involves empathy and humility. Vulnerability also equips you to take risks and adapt to change—and you cannot do either of those well without curiosity and resilience.

In this chapter, you will read stories of leaders who competed well *because* they led with heart and about some of the key strategic and tactical reasons behind their successes. At their core, all of these stories illuminate a unique interplay of intellect and heart, with intellect playing a vital support role in connecting leaders to the opportunity they were pursuing.

To reiterate what I said in the Introduction, responsive leaders are very focused on the people—the humanity—within the opportunity. Leading with heart allows them to live by the wisdom the civil rights activist Jesse Jackson offered "those at the top" when he said, "Never look down on anybody unless you're helping them up."

I begin this chapter with a story from the early days of my own career in top leadership roles. It's the story of how I felt I'd come home when I first encountered Dimock, despite its dilapidated buildings, depressed employees, and dire financial circumstances—and how that played out in the years that followed. My heart led me to a twenty-one-year experience of responsive leadership during which Dimock rose again to heights of respect and financial stability.

Later in the chapter, I also introduce my experiences at Wheelock College, where I served as president of a college that seemed more like Grade 13 when I got there. During my tenure, however, Wheelock grew to have an international presence and a curriculum that lured a diverse student population.

In the upcoming pages, we'll explore the practical lessons that leading with the heart teaches, the benefits such an approach has for an organization, and the signs that are apparent when you are leading with heart.

THE HEART OF DIMOCK

After I decided that I'd come home on Dimock's campus, the question was, "How can we resurrect this institution?"—the strategy question.

When I began my tenure as president and CEO, I first identified a goal of financial stability. Dimock's mission had always been clear: "to heal and uplift individuals, families, and our community." So now that my heart was engaged, I needed to put my intellect and skills behind it to build a team with whom I could create a strategic plan that led to sufficient funds to deliver services.

I took over at the height of the AIDS epidemic in 1983. The center welcomed people who were HIV-positive, in contrast to many other facilities. It's important to note that it was not until early 1985 that the conversation about heterosexual transmission of HIV was even part of the mainstream conversation. Before that, HIV was the plague of "homosexuals, intravenous drug users, hemophiliacs and Haitians who recently moved to the United States."[2] Dimock's healthcare activism with AIDS patients was not winning friends or donations; in fact, it was repulsive to some people.

I'm the type of person who becomes intensely driven by the environment I'm in. I envisioned potential, but I also saw the reality: a mottled reputation and receivership.

A turning point was when the board of trustees brought in an appraiser for the land. I read the report and wanted to cry. This is ten acres of land in a run-down part of the city, but I knew it was ten minutes from downtown and sat on a hill. That hill was adorned with beautiful old buildings—dilapidated, but beautiful. The report said that we should tear down the buildings and sell the land. It would be a great site for condos.

When I read that, I thought that Dr. Marie Zakrzewska, Linda Richards, and Mary Eliza Mahoney would be turning over in their graves.

Obviously, my heart kicked into high gear and drove my decision-making process to keep Dimock open and to honor the legacy of the men and women who built it.

Heart fuels passion, and passion can help you do important things, but it will not solve problems unless you draw the right complement of people to address the practical challenges ahead.

So my first job was to identify those people who were both qualified to help and in a position to do something substantial. My second job was to convince them that the institution had value.

I walked around the campus and came up with an idea about where to begin.

When you look at this building (on the next page), notice the turrets and other striking architectural detail. The slate roof and interior features add to its character and historic value. Why would we build condos when we had at least one building, if not more, that were qualified to be on the National Register of Historic Places, the official list of historic places worthy of preservation?

Stan Smith fell in love with this building, the original hospital at Dimock, and became critical in the fight to restore the center. He was Director of Historic Boston, an organization dedicated to preserving Boston's beautiful and historic buildings. He didn't care what we did at Dimock; he cared about the buildings. Sometimes a great ally has a completely different agenda that coincidentally supports yours. Consider the alliance between Winston Churchill and Joseph Stalin in World War II as shining example of that.

In just the first go-round, Stan Smith helped me raise a half-million dollars. It included money from charitable foundations and private sources like William Taylor, who was one of four generations of his family to run the *Boston Globe* and happened to be very interested in historic preservation. The *Boston Globe* itself became an investor in our rehabilitation efforts.

Historic Dimock Building

The experience of restoring Dimock was sustained by what I'll call *heart ticks*. These are moments and thoughts that reminded me of what I was aiming for. One of them was that I wanted Dimock to be good enough so that my mother could be a patient there and I would have total confidence in her care.

I knew that all of the pieces and parts of Dimock had value, but I didn't have a detailed, grand plan for how to bring these ten acres of old buildings back to life. Much of the process was incremental, and that reflected a response to circumstances and how rehabilitation of Dimock could occur organically. I never presented the board of trustees with a stack of slides that showed how we would first do A and then B, and then eventually, in a certain number of years, we would get to Z. That would *not* have been a leadership approach that was responsive to how the board and the rest of the Dimock organization related to progress. It was not an approach that would have motivated them or inspired them to take action to support me.

Responsive leadership meant going step by step, ensuring that the board and staff could see and feel incremental progress. Each step still had an element of risk, but we were steadily increasing everyone's comfort zone with each move forward. It was a matter of: "We fixed the roof. Now we have to renovate the building."

So when an opportunity arose that involved a much bigger step—and a much bigger risk—we were ready. The opportunity wandered onto the property in the form of two women with a plan to create a program for pregnant, incarcerated women. This was long before there was any national conversation about addressing the needs of both mother and child when the mother was serving time.

Conventional treatment of these women had been to remove the shackles long enough for them to have their babies and then immediately remove the babies from them and place the women back into their cells. The two women who came to me at Dimock based their program of medical care, parenting guidance, and job counseling on the belief that, for some women who've struggled with the law, having a baby can turn their lives around.

These women inquired about space. I pointed to a building that had been vacant for about fifty years. Squirrels and homeless people were living in it.

Together, we raised the money to renovate the building and launch the program. (We chased the squirrels out but did develop accommodations for the homeless people; that's another story!)

When we began the process of saving Dimock, the center cared for about 1,000 patients a year. After rehabilitating Dimock, we had an annual patient flow of about 36,000 people. It is just one of the metrics that illustrates how leading with heart can help make an organization more competitive.

WHAT DOES THE HEART TEACH?

Look up the definition of *heart* and you will find it described as a vital organ and as the innermost part of something. In the context of responsive leadership, let's define it as the vital organ of your decision-making, the central element of your day-to-day direction.

Most of us know what a broken heart teaches; experiencing loss helps us in self-discovery, it helps us appreciate connections with people who support us in rough times, and it helps us learn ways to bounce back, to find new paths to joy, and to move on. Keep all of these lessons in mind as we take a look at what the heart teaches you that is valuable to your leadership.

The Source of Your Happiness

My friend Maryann found herself dangling 400 feet above the ground, her heart racing, as she stared fearfully at the static climbing rope to which she was attached. This free rappel was the first section of the longest rope course ever created, and it was part of a 375-mile race in central Utah called the Eco-Challenge. Her team captain, descending on a rope a few feet from her, noticed that she was looking toward the rock face.

"Turn around," he yelled to her.

"No. I'll freak out."

"You need to see this view. You'll remember why we're here."

Maryann rotated, turning her eyes toward a vast expanse of sun-drenched hills and valleys. Excitement and gratitude immediately replaced her fear. This was why they decided to go into this grueling race. It was to experience intimately, like most people never could, the stunning beauty of this part of the American West.

Her heart was in the race because she could enjoy the wilderness with these four teammates who felt the way she did. The fact that they were getting next to no sleep, drinking contaminated water that they purified with iodine, taking huge physical risks, and eating only what they managed to stuff into their backpacks was inconsequential. They were happy.

When you go to work and, even on a bad day, something about what you are doing and where you are makes you feel good about yourself, you're probably in the right place—at least for now. Leading with the heart makes you consciously aware of what brings you joy and what stirs your passion.

The Role of Others

Two sets of people play a key role in your feelings of satisfaction with your leadership as well as your success in your role: the great leaders whose shoulders you stand on—the people who opened doors for you—and the people currently in your organization who you rely on so you can perform with excellence. These are the people you have the opportunity to open doors for.

One things I always tell audiences about leading in troubled times—a topic I'm asked to speak about quite a bit—is to surround yourself with the best people you can. Have the courage to let them do their jobs. When you hire people who are highly competent, and perhaps even smarter than you are, you can learn a great deal from them. And by investing in them and trusting them, even when they give you feedback you don't want to hear, you may well find that they exceed expectations in helping you succeed.

The systematic leadership I described in the Introduction does not necessarily exclude this approach to hiring, however, a systematic leader tends to impose a way of operating on an organization. Metaphorically, it is more like a garrison in which each soldier has a rank and a job and people might not feel empowered to be innovative or intellectually bold because it's above their pay grade. Such leaders have a way of doing things and that means you do your job their way, not yours.

In contrast, leading with heart is walking-the-hall leadership—you are in touch with the people around you, but you do not intrude on the way they operate in their own space. It is about responding to their need for direction, and being clear about the mission, without gutting their ability to function distinctively.

It is in your best interest, as well as theirs, to have them look forward to when they can stand on your shoulders and achieve their own greatness.

The Techniques of Resilience

When I first looked at the once-glorious buildings on the Dimock campus, I felt a kind of heartbreak. I could see someone had put great care, hope, and pride into those buildings, and demolishing them as part of a temporary fix to Dimock's financial problems would sadden me and many other people. The key word in that thought is *temporary*. When I pulled my thoughts together with my emotional response to the idea of condos on the campus, I realized I was being invited to be more resilient in my response—to come up with a long-term solution rather than a quick fix.

When Stan Smith entered the picture and brought his love of historical buildings and network of supporters into the discussion, I gained clarity about what to do to put Dimock on a path to permanent revival. I arrived at Dimock in 1983. By 1985, the entire campus had been placed on the National Register of Historic Places. With Stan Smith's help, we soon raised half a million dollars to put a new roof on the main hospital building and begin other restoration work.

And then, as the next section describes, we allowed ourselves to be radically optimistic and launched a fund-raising effort that has become legendary in Boston.

The Grace of Optimism

In 1987, the Dimock team committed to a major fund-raising event for the center. Typically, these types of events involve a high-priced dinner, maybe a high-profile speaker who will donate time for the cause, and a lot of fancy clothes. We had a different concept and were optimistic that, when people heard about it, they would still put on their fancy clothes, but they would also come to have fun.

Our vision was a tribute to Boston's jazz community, which exemplified the kind of diversity that Dimock embodied. Integral to that vision was an event that Dimock patients could afford to attend, not just board members and the wealthy philanthropic community in Boston.

We took over the entirety of Boston's Seaport World Trade Center and turned it into a series of jazz clubs representing Boston's great jazz legacy. No speeches, no sit-down dinner, just incredible music of all kinds throughout the World Trade Center. By the 90s, we were attracting about

3,000 people, dressed to the nines, for this event, representing the true diversity of the city. Over the years, the venue has changed and the format has been modified, but the intent remains the same—to celebrate the culture and diversity of the city. After thirty-one years, the 2018 Steppin' Out for Dimock raised over $1.3 million. During the lifetime of the event, over $30 million have contributed to keeping Dimock and its needed programs open.

At Steppin' Out, attendees came from different strata of Boston: corporate CEOs were on the dance floor with recovering addicts who had received treatment at Dimock and they didn't even know. We created the most diverse and exciting fundraising event in Boston.

As Steppin' Out quickly became the premiere fundraising event in the city, we had a unique opportunity to increase awareness of Dimock and to educate people about our mission and programs. The result was a significant influx of cash from the event, as well as major corporate support throughout the year.

You can use the heart to drive organizational change and sustain an optimism that keeps you going no matter what people say about your prospects for success. People who came to Steppin' Out in the early days, and who still come, were there to celebrate and support a great cause, not to be seen with celebrities and the social elite of Boston. Our hearts helped us stay true to the vision of an event that was inclusive for our staff, our patients, and our neighborhood—and at the same time, it raised lots and lots of money!

When It's Time to Let Go

When you are leading with heart, you are apt to periodically ask yourself, "Is staying in this position, with this organization, a healthy choice for the organization and its people?" Leading with head is more likely to provoke the question: "Is staying in this position, with this organization, a smart choice for *me*?"

Professor Andrew Henderson of the University of Texas has studied how long chief executives are optimally productive and he's concluded that many, if not most, hit a point when they should say goodbye: "People who get to the top tend to be both skilled and pretty fortunate, which gives them a certain level of self-confidence and makes them less open to new ways of thinking."[3] Jack Welch stayed in his senior role at General Electric for twenty years and then scooted out the door just as the company entered a decline. He looked heroic for the most part and sold a lot of books that passed along his wisdom, but one could argue that he did not do what was best for the organization in terms of a well-timed transition.

I wondered about staying at Dimock as long as I did, and did ask myself if staying was the best decision. The answer I came up with for many years was, obviously, "yes"—and then at the twenty-year mark, the answer turned to "no." Although Dimock will always have a place in my heart, leading with my heart told me when it was time to leave.

The next chapter is devoted to the lesson, "keep your bags packed." That chapter and the final chapter on transitions explore the reasons why and when a responsive leader should move on.

SIGNS YOU ARE LEADING WITH THE HEART

I wear a fitness tracker to remind myself to put one foot in front of the other because it's good for me. Throughout the day, I'll glance at it and maybe I'll get out of my chair and walk around the block because my numbers are a little low. In a similar way, signs that you are leading with your heart remind you that you are on a good path, with good intentions, so you need to keep moving. If you pay attention, your "numbers" won't be so low that you feel like a slug.

You Protect the Mission and Future of the Organization

Eyeing quarterly or even yearly results and then leaving when you miss the mark is the opposite of protecting the organization. Taking a higher paying and/or more prestigious job without regard for continuity or without seeing through a strategy you put in place is the opposite of protecting the organization. Acting recklessly in a way that jeopardizes the reputation of the company and its people is the opposite of protecting the organization.

In February 2003, I announced I would be leaving Dimock, but not until the spring of 2004. That gave the board ample time to recruit and for qualified candidates to put their resumes together, do their networking, and vie for the position. I didn't know where I was going to go—I wasn't rushing out the door to another organization—and that reality served the organization, and me, well. My tenure at Dimock had been a grand success and I would be leaving on a high note.

Deciding to leave Dimock in this way and with this timetable was one of those times when I checked my mental tracker and felt proud that I was going at a healthy pace.

You Make Your Mother (and Kids) Proud

There is more than one story behind this lesson, and all the stories have to do with the quality of your output.

When I first arrived at Dimock and looked at the medical facilities, I developed a conviction that I would help the staff bring the operation to a level where I would want my mother to be cared for there—and I would not just be okay with it, I would feel comfortable with every aspect of her care. Over time, I kept the "mother measure" in mind as the center steadily met increasingly higher standards and earned a national reputation for excellence.

When I first arrived at Wheelock, I took one look at the student cafeteria and realized I'd never let my kids eat there. I had an emotional response. The cafeteria symbolized a great failure of the institution in its services to students and I felt driven to change that. As the years went by at Wheelock, I kept looking around to make sure it was becoming the kind of place I would want my children to go to college.

You Listen More Than You Talk

When you listen, you support learning, conflict resolution, problem solving, and cultivation of trust. You cannot lead with the heart effectively unless you listen actively and often.

My introduction to Wheelock was being the commencement speaker in May 2003. At the time, I didn't know that the president of the college had decided to retire.

After announcing my upcoming departure from Dimock, I happened to have a meeting with a vice president of Blue Cross/Blue Shield (BC/BS). She quizzed me on my next move. When she realized I did not have that planned, she suggested *executive outplacement*, which involves companies offering their departing senior-level executives customized assistance in taking their next career step. Dimock didn't have the money for that and neither did I, so she got the president of BC/BS to agree to split the cost of outplacement coaching with me.

So, my first round of listening was hearing the results of tests and evaluations about where I should end up. I'm a mission-driven person, so certain areas surfaced as being likely to match my passions and interests, whereas others immediately fell off the radar. The problem was that one of the areas of great interest—higher education—did not match my experience.

That same May, just before I delivered the commencement address at Wheelock, I was on a panel about healthcare. During the discussion, I mentioned that I was leaving Dimock; a recruiter approached me afterward and said, "Let's have coffee." We had that coffee after my address and I found out that he was recruiting for positions in higher education.

Let's cut to the outcome: even though he told me I was not qualified to lead a four-year institution of higher learning, I put my hat in the ring and the board at Wheelock liked the looks of my hat. It certainly didn't hurt that the first time they heard my message and got a taste of my leadership was during my commencement address at their college.

Interestingly, Wheelock's mission statement was compatible with Dimock's, despite the fact that it was an educational rather than a medical institution. Founded as Miss Wheelock's Kindergarten Training School, Wheelock was dedicated "to improve the lives of children and families." I felt strongly that I could do the job of president if—and this was a big if—I had more practical knowledge of how to run a college.

So I did another major round of listening—this time to people who knew how to run a college. After nearly six months of interviews, I was finally offered the position of president in March 2004. Unfortunately, I wasn't invited to set foot on campus because the outgoing president still felt it was her turf. Therefore, between March and June, I tried to get up to speed by interviewing more than one hundred people in higher education—every college and university president in the Boston area who would speak to me and every former president of Wheelock.

The curiosity factor in the Big 4 had come to the fore.

When I arrived on campus as Wheelock's new president on July 1, 2004, I had plenty of listening practice, but I quickly turned my ears to students, as well as faculty and other staff. If I couldn't articulate the lesson before this point, I could certainly do it by the time I arrived on campus: God gave us one mouth and two ears, so do twice as much listening as talking.

3

Secret 3—

Keep Your Bags Packed

T here are two big reasons for incorporating the "keep
your bags packed" lesson into your leadership life.

- External influences have a profound impact on
  your ability to function optimally. You've made
  whatever contribution you can but are somehow
  constrained in doing more.

- Your values are being compromised. Certain ethics and principles are at the core of your leadership and influencers in your professional life want
  you to abandon or substantially modify them.

Whether you are part of a for-profit or not-for-profit organization, look at these two factors to determine whether
they are sources of whether those reasons are coming
into play:

- Money

- Power

On the surface, a message of "be ready to move on" sounds simple—but it isn't. Here's the simple part: you can be prepared to leave if your principles are violated, and you can be prepared to resign a position within your company if the atmosphere becomes corrosive or someone higher up wants to kick you out. The complicated part is when you're not prepared. It's not knowing whether you and your organization would be better off standing your ground and enforcing your principles rather than leaving. It's making the right call—stay and fight or depart gracefully—when your position is threatened. This chapter explores some clear-cut examples of why and when to leave and why and when to remain steadfast and entrenched. It also contains a case study that is more nuanced.

EXTERNAL INFLUENCES

Circumstances around you can change in ways that require you to move on. Politicians in the United States and most other democracies know this lesson well. Whether it is because of redistricting, swings in national priorities, a new voice in the presidency, or insufficient campaign funds, politicians have to be ready to move on. CEOs face shifts in board composition and slippage in market share as key external influences on their staying power. Anyone who depends on votes or quarterly returns to stay in a leadership role should have their bags packed at all times.

On a level more common to most leaders, the biggest external disruptor is a change in the person who has day-to-day authority over you. One week, you're productive and happy in your position leading the marketing efforts of a company; the next week, the new president of the company walks into his C-suite and you immediately update your resume.

Elon Musk, founder and CEO of Tesla, has a reputation for being mercurial, but more than that, he's an engineer and problem-solver at heart. If you are, too, and you work for him, that could be a problem if you want to hold on to your job. In April 2018, Musk became concerned that Tesla would fall short of first-quarter production forecasts, so he made a power play by removing his head of engineering and taking over the division himself.

Musk went on to set himself up as the victim of a power play when he locked horns with the US Securities and Exchange Commission (SEC). When he waffled on whether or not he had the financing to take the company private after announcing that he intended to do so, Musk was removed by his board from chairmanship for a three-year period to satisfy the SEC.

Money was the driver behind an organizational earthquake at a professional association that caught the leaders of four departments and their respective staff off guard. All of the senior people had been there for more than fifteen years and had built their division of the company into a profit center. They had been lulled into complacency, thinking their positions were secure, because they were making money for the company and enjoyed excellent reputations in their industry. The paradox is that their success was the reason for them losing their jobs.

The new company president preferred the business focus of a different division—one that was losing money. He convinced the board that infusing that division with capital would ultimately be a strong business move with tremendous income potential. Because he was new, he had a certain cachet with the board that an old familiar face may not have had. His plan to get the funding? Sell the profitable division to a competitor with deep pockets.

One Thursday morning, he called the two dozen employees together and delivered the message, "You will no longer have a job in two weeks." That announcement caused a profound sense of disorientation and a series of long lunches involving alcoholic beverages.

Only one of the division leaders had kept her bags packed. She knew she worked in a volatile industry and, in the course of twenty-one years with the company, had seen how dramatically a new president could impact the structure and operation of the organization. Without missing a beat, she contacted key people in her network and made it known that she intended to stay with the industry and join another organization. She knew the first principle of responsive leadership, which I talked about in the Introduction: she led herself first.

This story has many lessons, of course, and it resurfaces later, but it is presented with the president as the point of focus.

An article entitled "The Board Just Fired Me . . . and I'm the Founder!" by a woman known only as Anonymous captures what has happened to many senior executives through the years. These are people who assumed they were untouchable, therefore, they paid no attention to the signs related to money and power that could have given them a heads-up about leaving—or dramatically changing course. The following is a section of that article entitled "Should Have Seen the Signs":

> *I should have seen the signs. But I didn't. Looking back now, I can pinpoint when the shift in board personality began:*

about 6 years ago. There was an evolution of the board from a group of enthusiastic, flexible individuals to a collection of people who engage in inwardly-focused groupthink. They were unwilling to engage in any sort of healthy debate. They consistently ignored the financial warning signs I pointed out, and they flat-out saw only limited responsibility for themselves to be fundraisers.

Nearly three years ago I missed another piece of evidence. A long-time board member remarked that boards should have executive sessions at every meeting—without the CEO. And so they did.

Most important, they did not seem to grasp the fact that our mission required a mix of charitable and earned income. They believed that if we could just figure out the right business model we could survive on earned income alone.

The result? When they finally paid attention to the financial situation of the organization, they panicked.[1]

Even if you think everyone at the company adores you, keep your eyes open for shifts related to money and power that could bring with them a movement to oust you. As I will explore in greater depth in Chapter 8, my experience at Wheelock went from a decade of success to a situation in which board priorities and composition shifted, with the board sometimes convening without my involvement or going into unscheduled executive sessions. Changes like that mean your job security is gone.

COMPROMISED VALUES

Sometimes courageous leadership can get you in trouble, so if you are more likely to speak up than shut up, keep your bags packed.

John Oscar Boone, Sr. was the first African American to head the Massachusetts Prison System, making him the first African American to head *any* major state prison system in the United States. His background made him well qualified to effect the kind of reform that the state system needed. I thought it was particularly interesting that Massachusetts chose him because it was, and still is, a state where most of the color is concentrated in the city of Boston.

I went to hear him speak and remember the leadership lesson he passed along that became the subject of this chapter. Boone said that in order to be effective in your job, keep your bags packed. You cannot do your work when you fear losing your job. If you do, you will lack the courage to do what's right.

In the relatively short time that Boone held the position of commissioner of corrections, "He was credited for transforming the Massachusetts Prison System by pushing feverishly to ensure humane conditions for inmates and the availability of rehabilitation programs to keep the incarcerated of all races out of the system once they were released back into society."[2]

Despite his accomplishments, however, Boone ruffled the wrong feathers when he tried to break up the patronage system, among other things. His values always led him before any career stability or advancement. In that sense, he had a great deal in common with his younger brother, Joseph Boone, a civil rights activist who marched with Martin Luther King Jr. and spearheaded the successful movement that led to the integration of lunch counters and department stores in Atlanta.

Courage is often a high-risk proposition, but if you make decisions based on what others who can cause you to lose your job will think of you, then you diminish your effectiveness as a leader.

In *Business Lessons from the Edge,* author Jim McCormick, who helps CEOs create a healthy risk culture, offers three reasons why a leader would want to conduct herself with integrity. They center on the practical value of never compromising your values.

- *Stay true to your moral compass.*

- *Establish that you can be trusted in a business deal.*

- *Protect your reputation.*

If you accept those reasons, what non-negotiables do you need to establish to achieve those objectives? That is, how do you define your own integrity? General examples of non-negotiables would include the kinds of business dealings you would hate to encounter in others: willfully misrepresenting facts, capabilities, and statements and overpromising while underdelivering.

Very simply, stay true to what you know to be right and get that clear in your head with as much specificity as you require to adhere to a strategy of integrity.[3]

McCormick concludes the section with a statement that I would also like to make my own in this context: "If you don't know what's right, you have bigger problems than we can address in this book."[4] The step that precedes having the courage to lead in accordance with your values is therefore identifying what those values are. Make a list of things about which you will not compromise. If you have that in your desk drawer in addition to your heart and your head, then you will be fully prepared to meet any ethical dilemma that comes along. You will have a personal and professional canon of ethics to guide you away from compromise and toward complete commitment to doing what is right.

Issues of money and power were ever-present during my presidency at Wheelock. The critical background includes that I was a nontraditional president, not just for Wheelock when I took the helm in 2004, but also for any institution of higher learning. I had no formal experience in higher education administration, having spent my entire professional career in health and mental health executive leadership positions. I was the first African American president in the College's 115-year history. And I was only its third woman president, even though this institution was founded by a woman, Lucy Wheelock, in 1886 and was a women's college for most of its history.

I joined the Wheelock community *because of my values*, so even though they were frequently challenged, I felt I had a strong centering force while I was there. I believed in the college's compelling mission: to improve the lives of children and families. I came to Wheelock because I believe deeply in higher education and its power of to lift people out of poverty to places where they can change communities and society as a whole for the better. I was also fascinated by the challenges facing small independent private colleges and the good that these institutions have done for individuals and communities. And I was intrigued by the challenges inherent in today's very complex academic environment.

Whether it was about budgeting, strategic planning, tenure criteria, shared governance, student behavior, or admissions decisions—all money and power issues—individuals and groups within the administration, faculty, and senior staff were not, and could not be, always on the same page. We were challenged by our different understandings and views of what values were at stake—what was the "right" thing to do, what was the fair decision, whether equality or equity should prevail, which competing goals should take precedence in fulfilling the college's mission.

One responsive leader who prevailed heroically in this environment of higher education—and carried her bags out the door only when she was good and ready!—is Ruth Simmons. Simmons was the eighteenth president of Brown University and the first African American president of any Ivy League university.

Brown was initially funded by slave traders, but rather than brush that dust under the rug, Simmons took a series of bold actions to give Brown a progressive, inclusive image. It was actually far more than just image: the first thing she did was change the prospects for acceptance at Brown dramatically.

Simmons' initiative was radical: she aimed to institute need-blind admission, which would remove the ability to pay from the admissions equation. Despite that values-based commitment, she hit a point early on when university administrators told her it wouldn't work. There just wasn't enough money to carry it off.

Simmons stood her ground. She neither backed down, nor did she leave her position. She got seed money for the bold program by locking in a roughly $100 million donation from Sidney Frank, a 1942 graduate of Brown who made billions through his investments in Grey Goose vodka and Jägermeister.

Other incidents followed that looked as though they might be her undoing. Behaving in a manner consistent with her values made Simmons a target again and again.

Race became an issue after she appointed a faculty committee to research Brown's historic ties to slavery and to recommend ways it might acknowledge and memorialize that past. "She wants to pay reparations!" people falsely said. There were battles over ROTC and over the future of athletics at Brown, and there was a nasty disagreement with the near-bankrupt city of Providence over the amount of the University's contributions to the municipal budget.[5]

Simmons admitted that her values, and the actions that gave them life at Brown, had roots in her background: "I think if you've been mired in poverty at any juncture and you get to know the capabilities of the people in very poor communities, you're the first person to recognize that there is as much talent and brilliance in that community as in any other."[6]

Do an about face and take a walk with me on the dark side now. This is the path that leaders devoid of a moral compass take. These are leaders who don't keep their bags packed because they seem to feel that the only values worth having *are* money and power.

A classic example involves the BP executives who treated the *Deepwater Horizon* disaster like a financial and legal inconvenience despite the fact that the blowout caused the loss of human life and almost incalculable environmental damage. In short, on April 10, 2010, a catastrophic failure of blowout prevention equipment on board the massive offshore rig led to the fouling of an extensive region of the Gulf of Mexico and ended the lives of eleven men. BP CEO Tony Hayward made his values, and the values of BP's board and other senior leaders, abundantly clear when he made the following statements:

April 29, 2010: "What the hell did we do to deserve this?"[7]

May 13, 2010: "The Gulf of Mexico is a very big ocean. The amount of volume of oil and dispersant we are putting into it is tiny in relation to the total water volume."[8]

*May 18, 2010: "I think the environmental impact of this
disaster is likely to be very, very modest."[9]*

*May 31, 2010: "There's no one who wants this over more
than I do. I would like my life back."[10]*

Regarding the last comment, Hayward got his life back
when he was abruptly replaced by Bob Dudley, who took
over as CEO the following July and headed the plea deal
negotiations that led to a scapegoating exercise involving
three long-time employees—a continuation of the apparent tradition of this company of compromising standards
whenever profits are endangered.[11]

Hayward was forced to pack his bags, leaving behind
an annual salary of $1.5 million, but he was still covered
by a $17 million pension. Money and power were "values"
that served him well—up to the point of being humili-
ated in the media and discarded by his employer.

In summary, success of courageous leadership can have
two very different outcomes. One involves a leader like
Ruth Simmons rising to almost legendary status through
her resilience and moral conviction, and the other with a
leader standing his ground and finding no alternative to
walking away, as in the case of John Boone.

If you are courageous, you may not always win in the
short run, but you will always win in the long run.

BAGS PACKED, BUT STAYING PUT

The clash between a leader's values and those of powers-
that-be need not result in resignation or firing, as Ruth
Simmons proved with her need-blind initiative at Brown
University. My story of an analogous fight involved a
major project that took some of Wheelock's students and
faculty off campus and into a community with dire service

needs. The questions from detractors that were meant to shake the ground under me related to the academic value of the effort and the investment of resources.

Mayor Thomas Menino of Boston had decided that the city's financial troubles required cutting certain programs and rethinking how to fund others. In the spring of 2010, Boston Centers for Youth & Families began implementing its new strategic plan to consolidate eight of its then forty-six community centers to eliminate duplication and to try to keep the remaining centers active and providing vital services. Unfortunately, there was no more city money to fund any of them.

Wheelock's director of college sports-based youth initiatives at the time caught wind of the dilemma and approached me about the possibility of Wheelock partnering with the city to manage and staff one of the centers.

I jumped in with both feet. This opportunity was consistent with the kind of community-focused program I felt was essential for the college. We were part of the city— we took up space in the city, we drew students from the city—and yet we had been disconnected in some ways. Putting ourselves to work at a youth center would mean our students could learn from the community, launch educational and athletic programs for the community, do research, and make a difference in families' lives.

Not everyone agreed with me, however. Although many at the college felt strongly that the college should be doing this, on the far end of the criticism, powerful, tenured faculty members and some members of the board of trustees saw this as a diversion of resources and a contamination of our higher education programs rather than as an enhancement of them.

Rather than wasting time arguing, I made my case for the reasons and benefits of the program and then moved ahead promptly. Before anyone could get in our way, a team of us from Wheelock visited the eight centers. Our hearts were soon set on working with the one with the most desperate needs and, coincidentally, with the greatest diversity. Actually, *my* heart was set on it, and as Marta Rosa, a cochair of the leadership team for the project, recently reminded me, "We laughed when you picked Mattahunt. Picking the one with the greatest need was pretty much what we expected from you." The Mattahunt Community Center had been plagued by deficits, was surrounded by a community that had lost interest in it, and occupied a building that not only lacked creature comforts, but also presented safety hazards to people.

Mayor Merino was very receptive to the idea of a partnership—which, notably, included zero funding from the city. Marta and I spearheaded the planning process so that we could sort out exactly what a partnership with the city would look like if there was no money involved. The Mayor offered his name and said he would make calls to funding sources we identified, but the city would not be issuing any checks for the project. In other words, it was a partnership of ideals.

The reality of no city funding was, of course, ammunition for the critics on campus, some of whom were happy to jump to the conclusion that our efforts to raise funds for the center would endanger their possibilities for funds from the same sources.

That didn't happen. We raised private funds that never would have come to the college. Funding sources included The Boston Foundation (TBF) and the United Way, neither of which was a candidate for giving grants to Wheelock. TBF supports nonprofit organizations that take action to help the city. The United Way addresses problems around the world like access to healthcare, children's basic education needs, and homelessness.

With the success of our fundraising, we were well on the way to silencing the naysayers, but there was only one victory that needed to occur so that no one's job or reputation was put at risk: the programs we put in place at the center had to thrive. That meant substantial community participation as well as coordination with the Mattahunt Public Elementary School, which is where the center was located. To complicate matters, the school had just been downgraded to a Level 4 school, meaning it was an underperforming school that was struggling to meet student needs. As a result, student performance was well below levels of many other schools—exactly the kind of students who needed a youth center including enhanced academic programs.

Marta's extensive interviews with people in the community ensured that we were in touch with the concerns, expectations, and aspirations of the people Mattahunt was supposed to serve. Her work effectively laid a foundation of trust between Wheelock and the community, and as she later said, "The success of the project was that we started by learning about the community. We asked, 'What are the assets of this community?' not just 'What are the needs of this community?'"[12]

The next step was a seven-month process of organizing in the community to get families to feel ownership of the center. Eighty adults from the community participated in the planning process as well as children who drew pictures of what they wanted to see in the center. Marta and her team made sure they were an integral part of the progress in developing programs and revitalizing the center. Volunteers poured in; Governor Deval Patrick even helped us paint the place.

With the influx of community people, arguments against Wheelock's participation steadily weakened. Most of the critics who said we were putting limited resources in the wrong place had a change of heart and mind. Faculty who wanted to participate joined forces with the people served by Mattahunt. Students, particularly those majoring in social work, interned at the center. They provided services and conducted field research. It could never be argued that this project stole time from their academic experience; it gave their studies meaningful depth. The center also drew other groups who began providing services to the community to complement what Wheelock brought to it.

Mattahunt would open in the afternoon to ensure that kids had a place to go after school and would stay active into the evening. To sustain a high level of activity—going from serving thirty kids to about one hundred in the after-school program alone—we had to raise between $350,000 and $400,000 a year.

The last remaining critics who continued to hammer away at us four or five years into a six-year effort maintained that Wheelock was becoming too much of a social service organization instead of an academic institution. That was an indefensible argument since our international footprint and student population continued to grow.

With Mattahunt we won a practical and a moral victory. My packed bags and I did not have to leave the campus—at least not this time.

The simple truth is that you cannot lead effectively and boldly if you are not passionate about the mission and organization. But if you remain passionate and are standing shoulder to shoulder with people who share your commitment and values, then think about the merits—and perhaps the necessity for the good of the organization—of staying right where you are.

4.

Secret 4—
Stay on Point in the Midst of Risk

B ill Clinton once said, "Being president is like running a cemetery: you've got a lot of people under
you and nobody's listening."[1] Well, you can't wake the
dead, but as a leader, you have the challenge of getting
all of the living beings around you to hear your message.

This chapter offers you insights on presenting messages effectively, reaching skeptics in your target audience, inspiring people to act in response to your message,
and creating a bridge to your subsequent message and
agenda. As a responsive leader, you will handle the challenge of skeptics and calls to action differently from people who have an I say–you do mentality. The guidance
is illuminated by examples from industry, ministry, and
my own experience convincing the Wheelock Board of
Trustees and greater Wheelock community to undertake
its first architectural addition in sixty years. This chapter
is also supported by Appendix B, which features communications tools and techniques—specific guidance on
how to stay on point.

MASTERING THE POINT

When Steve Jobs launched the iPhone, he ostensibly bundled three big announcements, but he had a singular point: we have a new way to connect you to people and content.

He opened with this statement: "This is a day I've been looking forward to for two and a half years. Every once in a while, a revolutionary product comes along that changes everything."[2]

With those words, his introduction of the iPhone did more than build excitement for his audience: he sent chills of anticipation and longing up and down their spines.

Jobs used history well to stick with his point. He cited the revolution in computing that the 1984 introduction of the Macintosh personal computer provoked and then noted the importance of the 2001 introduction of the iPod that "changed the entire music industry." The manipulative—and I mean this in the most positive way—aspect of spotlighting this history is that the audience was set up to accept as success anything that followed it!

But Steve Jobs then used the method of communicating a single message to bring his audience to thunderous applause. Again and again, he repeated what he called three "revolutionary" products—at first blush, three different things—that were being launched that day. With a rotating cube projected behind him that displayed the icons of the iPod, iPad, and Safari browser, he said:

So, three things. A widescreen iPod with touch control. A revolutionary mobile phone. And a breakthrough internet communications device.

An iPod. A phone. And an internet communicator.

An iPod. A phone. Are you getting it?

These are not three separate devices. This is one device.[3]

One device? Jobs' audience at that presentation on January 9, 2007, went nuts. There is really no other way to describe how excited they were about a single new product that would deliver so much "revolution." They didn't just say "hello" to the iPhone, they said, "Hallelujah!"

Contrast the way Jobs mastered the message with the way Google cofounder Sergey Brin mangled his.

The launch of Google Glass began with the words, "We're going to do something pretty magical here and we have a special surprise for you."[4] Recall that Jobs opened with the present tense: he talked about something here and now. Saying, "we're going to do something" means the big thing—whatever it is—hasn't happened yet. That alone is enough to undermine a message. Consider if someone said, "I'm going to forgive you" or "I forgive you." Which would you believe had more sincerity behind it?

For the next four minutes of the launch event, which seemed like a lifetime due to Brin's rambling banter that told the audience almost nothing about the product, he used words like *amazing* to describe what was to come in the demonstration of Google Glass. We could legitimately say that Brin's singular message was "Google Glass is amazing." It was repeated, but unlike Jobs' repetition that the iPhone was one device with three key features, Brin's repetition of *amazing* fell flat. To make the launch even worse, the wow-moment involved skydivers wearing Google Glass on their descent to a rooftop in San Francisco—not so "wow" for the millions of YouTube fans had who already seen the same kind of sights recorded by wireless GoPro cameras. More than eleven minutes into the presentation,

Brin finally introduced someone who could talk about the features of Google Glass. It was an inauspicious beginning for a product that failed in the marketplace. It was a New Coke of high technology.

Mastering a point starts with refining your message to a distinct idea. After that, you need to plan how you will say it multiple times in a number of places. You might have to convey the message fifty times before your audience gets it: you might say it in the board meeting, in individual meetings, in casual conversation, and to other people while a board member is within earshot.

It's important to achieve clarity with that single, cohesive message rather than try to adorn it with other messages that may distract from the core point. In other words, *beware of tangents* when you intend to persuade your audience about something important, or even transformative. Also, beware of adjectives and adverbs. Jobs' message about the iPhone was "one device, three functions" whereas Brin's was "Google Glass is amazing." As soon as words such as *incredible, magical,* and *amazing* become part of a message, your radar should go off. "Google Glass is wearable technology" is a more powerful statement because it conveys accurate information about what the product is. It sets expectations and arouses curiosity more than *amazing* does. The listener automatically wants to know "Where is it worn?" "What does it do?"

Keeping a conversation, a speech, or a panel discussion in focus requires effort and energy and demands a strong command of the subject matter. If you jump from one subject to another, you convey a couple of major weaknesses: 1) an apparent desire to skip away from the subject at hand for some reason and 2) an inability to keep your conversation tightly linked to the main subject.

The common outcome is that you lose your audience, or at the very least, you confuse them.

Take the lessons of Jobs and Brin—and others in the spotlight who either communicate notably well or notably poorly—into your own environment. Actually, let me share with you how I brought them to life in mine. My "Steve Jobs moment" was not about a global shake-up in communications, but rather an idea for creating a huge opportunity for a college that desperately needed a vision for the future. If I could convince our board that constructing a new building—after zero construction for six decades—was a gigantic opportunity, then this was my iPhone moment.

The student cafeteria at Wheelock was in the basement of an old building; it was literally the pits.

As I mentioned in Chapter 1, one of my standards for where I work is that I want it to be good enough for my family. That was the measure I used for the medical facilities at Dimock when I asked myself, "Would I want my mother to be treated here?" Similarly, at Wheelock, I told the board that my standard for any part of the campus would be that it was good enough for my children.

When I saw the cafeteria, I asked myself, "Would I want my kids to eat here?" My head rumbled, "No way!" The cafeteria was old, dirty, dingy, and in a basement—it was depressing.

I told the board we had to build a state-of-the-art student center with a cafeteria that had windows. I began to make the case that students would feel more inclined to enroll at Wheelock if they shared their pizza with sunlight.

We needed a building that would change our ability to function in the present and be successful in the foreseeable future. A simple concept like "we must give Wheelock a new building" was as transformative for our college community as "one device, three functions" was for the world.

The board of trustees was scared. Transformative ideas create excitement and optimism, but they also generate reluctance and fear. They could not predict the outcome because this was new, high-risk territory for them. Uniformly, they recognized the building venture would have huge consequences, and most were on the side of optimism, yet some were held back by gnawing skepticism.

We needed $9 million to accomplish the goal of planning and preparation, including design, but more than $36 million for total execution of the project. Without an investment like this, I saw our program of boosting enrollment failing, or at least faltering. I needed to communicate my distinct message about what would happen after we built the new student center, and that bridge message (a concept discussed later in this chapter) was basically "build it and they will come." So, in addition to presenting the case to the board, I had what I called fireside chats à la Franklin Delano Roosevelt—I had small groups of board members meet with me in a comfortable area near a fireplace.

At those chats, even more than at the board meetings, I heard certain members perk up and say, "What are we afraid of?" That generated even more conversations about the message.

"Same message, multiple venues, multiple times" is embedded in the curriculum of seminaries, too, because spiritual leaders obviously need to know how to persuade people. Clergy learn that whether the issue is bingo in the basement or the power of God's love throughout the world, the congregation has to hear and see the message many times.

Carolyn Wills, a retired United Methodist Church (UMC) pastor who earned her Doctor of Divinity from Nazarene Theological Seminary, notes,

> *The accepted premise is that it takes at least six times to have a message stick with people. This is why a turkey dinner at the church social hall will be announced before services, announced after services, listed in the weekly bulletin, featured in a poster on the wall, advertised on the church website, and mentioned in phone calls to members.*[5]

As for the spiritual messages, the approach to "multiple times" is codified in a book called the *lectionary*, used in Christian churches, but analogous guides cycle through spiritual readings in Judaism and Islam, as well. On any given Sunday, pastors following the lectionary will have thematically coordinated readings—a couple from the Old Testament and a couple from the New Testament—they will preach about the same central message in the sermon; and they will give the person in charge of music guidance on ensuring the hymns reinforce that message. Again, that's six times and six ways the congregation is theoretically hearing the same message.

What can you do if you have an approach to handling information that seems to lead you off the trail? If you're like the hiker who wants to check out every interesting flower and rock on the side of the road, you might be a very creative person and a scintillating conversationalist, but you have to know when to abandon that tendency in favor of a more streamlined approach to communicating.

In Appendix B, I offer some *Tools of Structure*, which are tools and techniques to keep yourself on the path to accomplishing your goals. To foreshadow, the discussion centers on

- Agenda

- Reports supporting the agenda

- An organizing procedure for meetings

- A "lectionary" for messaging

A *point* is commonly defined as the tapered, sharp end of a tool. If your tool is conversation or presentation, then the sharp end is your message.

REACHING THE SKEPTICS

Getting your message heard by people who are not inclined to applaud your efforts connects you to people who are potential opponents—but who might come to support you, or at least not get in your way, if what you say resonates with them. Sure, it's easy to win them over once you've proven beyond the proverbial shadow of a doubt that your message foreshadowed a successful venture. However, getting the skeptics to either shut up or come over to your side *before* that success is a victory of messaging.

Steve Jobs was remarkable for getting people on board with his technology vision, however, when he made his on-point launch presentation of the iPhone, a number of critics tried to spoil the optimism for Apple lovers. Not being what I would call a responsive leader—he was a visionary, not a leader—how did his messaging help convert the skeptics? He had apostles who took the well-crafted singular message of the iPhone and preached the gospel of "three in one" to both fans and critics. What they learned by listening to both sets of people also helped them refine the product. One of my friends who worked for Apple on and off as a consultant and a staffer told me the company had an official name for the people on staff who did this: technology evangelists. Apple still maintains a cadre of technology evangelists for their various product divisions and lists as one of the job requirements that they "believe in Apple" (as would be expected of an evangelist of any faith).[6]

Jobs engendered responsive leadership at Apple through his passion, clarity of purpose, and ability to deliver on promises. Those leaders within the company listened to consumers, built teams, respected the values that motivated people, and ultimately contributed substantially to the success of a good product.

The reality is that, within three months of the iPhone's release, more than 1.5 million units had sold for $499 each. The people who thought it performed well spread Jobs' message of "one device, three functions" and ultimately, they nearly silenced the skeptics, like Microsoft CEO Steve Ballmer. Without realizing it, even Ballmer helped promote Jobs' message of "one device, three functions" when he criticized it:

> *So should you buy an iPhone? Sure, if you want to own a beautifully designed phone/Internet device/music player and are willing to put up with some occasionally exasperating problems. Everyone else, especially those who already rely on a PDA phone for messaging, should probably wait.*[7]

This is a true victory of messaging. Even Jobs' most vocal and high-profile opponent told the world what made the product unique.

I think Steve Jobs did not care if he converted anyone. He had clarity and singularity in his message and complete conviction that his product fulfilled his technological vision. He probably knew that both his staff evangelists and early adopters of the iPhone (who effectively became evangelists) would reach the skeptics. The message of a unique and excellent product would ripple across conversations and create a wave of acceptance.

Jobs was a curious and imaginative man who sometimes reached the skeptics by proposing what seemed like outrageous objectives. He is one of the many prominent figures throughout history who had the courage to invite his critics to yell, "That can't be done!" with the more powerful effect of energizing people to get "it" done. When John F. Kennedy gave his moon speech to Congress in 1961, that is exactly what many people said—and they were the ones who made sense, because Kennedy had no plan to land on the moon. And yet, thanks to people who rose to the challenge, the United States did land on the moon before the decade was over.

I heard the same kind of critical noise when I proposed that we build a new student center at Wheelock. We had a campus green on the Riverway, a beautiful street running along the Muddy River, which is a protected public area surrounded by hiking trails and small parks. When I suggested we build on it, a chorus of voices on the board and faculty said, "That can't be done!" because of Boston's historic preservation policies.

I was curious: Was it a myth that no one could build there, or was it true? Getting your facts straight is a critical first step in a major project, particularly if you know you are going to face opposition. Your own passion for a project heightens when you know the facts are on your side.

We talked with the preservation organization and various people within city government; our research told us, "Yes, we *could* do it." People who assume that what they've heard about the impossibility of a project is true will often not even do the homework required to validate (or invalidate) their assumptions. They don't try to see if the goal is achievable.

Once it was clear that no city ordinance or preservation group had the power to block us legally from building, our task force aimed high aesthetically. If Wheelock was going to build on this prominent location, then the building had to enhance the view and not detract from it. Integral to that vision was the concept that this building should symbolize the fact that Wheelock was looking toward the future, that we were moving forward.

The more I talked about what could be, and why this building represented the commitment of our college to excellence, the more the skeptics fell silent. The last to mute their criticism were those who felt this project would divert resources from academic programs. They said very little after someone on the board got excited enough about the building to write a check for $1 million. That was enough to hire a first-class architect, do soil testing, and make myriad other preparations to build.

In summary, reaching the skeptics is a step-by-step process involving

- Getting your facts straight

- Reinforcing the core message and vision among people who can help you spread the word—that is, consistently expanding the circle of people who will help you reach the skeptics

- Getting clarity on the key objections and criticisms

- Countering those objections and criticisms with actions

Each step you take along the way creates the environment for long-term success. Identifying the small steps, and putting them in a logical sequence, will give you the leap forward you need to achieve the vision.

INSPIRING TO ACTION

The final point in the preceding bulleted list refers to events such as the board member getting excited enough to donate $1 million. He heard the message over and over and finally did more than embrace it: he helped give it life.

His donation then inspired further action. With the issue of planning funds handled, board members who questioned the project solely on the basis of resources turned the corner. The skeptics were saying, "Wow, this might happen!" More and more voices spread a message of "This building represents the future of the college." As a result, when we issued the request for proposals to architectural firms, we had famous architects bidding to design the new student center for little ol' Wheelock.

Our choice was William Rawn, an award-winning designer who did the Seiji Ozawa Hall at Tanglewood, Swarthmore College Residence Halls, W Boston Hotel and Residences, and many other gorgeous and notable structures. Bill Rawn's firm then helped us energize students and faculty to care about the project by inviting them to share their design ideas through a *charrette*. Technically, this refers to a period of time focused on design and planning, but it also involves meetings to engage stakeholders in the design process. It was coordinated by the architectural firm, which brought in materials and sketches to stimulate ideas. Many people plunged into their designs and descriptions with so much vigor that they had a vision of what would hang on the walls. One of the biggest skeptics in the beginning was a board member who ultimately submitted a detailed concept for a grand brick-and-stone building reminiscent of Ivy League schools—complete with a fireplace. Even the mayor of Boston had his vision of what the building should look like.

Having such a noteworthy architect at the helm inspired action in another, very important way: suddenly, people found their checkbooks because they were thrilled to have their names associated with a Rawn-designed building. They flocked to fundraising dinners where Bill Rawn spoke about his designs and the plans for Wheelock. People sat up straight in their chairs: architecturally, the Wheelock community was in the big leagues.

Ultimately, the design we erected in a mere two years was a modern, glass-and-steel, 66,000 square-foot building. From the student center on the glass-enclosed bottom floors, it gives students a view of the river on one side and an urban view on the other. The upper three floors are residences. The dejected feeling I had when I first walked on campus and saw the dingy basement cafeteria was replaced with elation at knowing that students in the new cafeteria would look out at the river, through the tops of trees, and have the perception that they were eating in a forest. Finally, they had sunlight with their pizza.

Just entering the cafeteria gave them a sense of pride. The architect believed that every building should have a grand element, no matter how utilitarian the building was meant to be. The concept is that the element conveys the energy of the structure. In the Wheelock Campus Center and Student Residence, the grand element was a staircase that lead to the cafeteria, which occupied the second floor.

With the building a reality, people waited in line to have their events there. They wanted to claim the class-room in the building. They wanted to live and study there.

The building itself inspired the board, faculty, and students to take action to move Wheelock several notches up in its standing within the academic community.

BRIDGING TO THE NEXT MESSAGE

Once you manage to convey your message well, reach the ears of the skeptics, and arouse people around you to take action, your next communications challenge is to take the momentum you created and move on to the next topic on your agenda. With Steve Jobs and the second generation of iPhone, the message was "now supporting third-party applications." Again, the point was specific and fact-based. iPhone OS 2 wasn't described as merely "amazing" or "the latest and greatest." It was described as supporting third-party apps. Listeners could hear that and say, "I get it." Immediately after that, they wonder exactly what you want them to wonder: What's next?

I learned from my mentors that you can't do every-thing at once. Staging progress is a big part of leadership excellence.

The optimism part of leadership is that there is going to be a next project. There is going to be a future. There is going to be another success—and you will be part of it. In the meantime, be patient and maintain the success of what we have already accomplished . . . and stay tuned for further updates!

At Wheelock, the success of the campus center made it clear how urgently other buildings needed either dramatic upgrades or replacement. But at that point, rather than feel desperate and question our ability to accomplish these projects, we could move forward with confidence: "We can do this." We were also seeing an uptick in enrollment, so my bridge message of "build it and they will come" was also coming to life.

A message like "One by one, until we're done" then became realistic, and we had far fewer skeptics picking at the logic of our progress. Campus-wide, a tidal wave of enthusiasm for bringing Wheelock physically into the twenty-first century corresponded with a commitment to bring the academic program into the new millennium.

It is always important to choose your next project carefully, rather than just take the easiest or most attractive possibility. At Wheelock, we saw that there were faculty in office spaces that were as depressing as the old basement cafeteria. If we were going to move our entire operation into the new century, we couldn't have our professors surrounded by nineteenth-century dust. With the evolving message of "moving into the new century," we built a state-of-the-art technology center and moved those faculty members into the top floor of the new building.

When bridging to the next message, your job is logically building on the fulfillment of the last one. Too many technology companies—and we can cite Google and Google Glass as an example—have tried to build on the great success of a product or service without fully thinking through what their constituents needed. Not necessarily what loud voices said they wanted, but what their core constituency felt they *needed*. If we start with Aristotle, move forward to Sigmund Freud, and even farther forward to self-improvement coach Anthony Robbins, we hear lots of evidence that people will do much more to avoid pain than they will to seek pleasure. The point is, if you give people what they need to avoid an uncomfortable situation, you can get them on your side very quickly. It's important to consider this in your next-step priorities, just as we did in taking our faculty out of the basement at Wheelock right after we took the students out of it.

Now let's say you didn't quite hit the mark. What then? How do you bridge to the next message when the number of skeptics has increased due to some measure of failure? Let's take a look at the turnaround success of a famous entrepreneur for an illustration of how to jump over the critics and keep running toward a major accomplishment.

Arianna Huffington launched *The Huffington Post* in 2005 when lots of people thought she was nothing more than the spoiled former wife of Republican congressman Michael Huffington. Her business model of an online magazine with unpaid bloggers was ridiculed from both a financial and an editorial perspective. However, her instincts and business savvy told her that she should keep inviting people with genuine expertise to contribute and that readers who wanted and needed what they offered would return to her site. She believed in the fresh voices and the expertise and energy behind them. By 2009, she became #12 in *Forbes'* list of Most Influential Women in Media, moving up later to become one of the most influential people in the world.

A more relatable example comes from a friend who raised money for a children's museum and learning center in a city that had been scarred by race riots. Her boss, the founder of the museum, told her to keep hammering on the fact that their facility was the only safe haven for dozens of latchkey kids in the area who had nowhere to go after school. Simple message: "We give the kids after-school fun and learning." The organization was able to raise millions for the building, a computer lab, and other projects, but this one program was unfunded. My friend's boss told her to camp out in certain offices until she got the money to fund the program. Ultimately, camping out and repeating her message got the funding from the Hearst Foundation. That would not have happened without the previous successes of the organization, however. Her job was to build a bridge between what others had said and done, what the after-school program offered, and what potentially lay ahead for both.

No matter what phase of your communications challenge you happen to be in, you are always dealing with skeptics. Given facts, skeptics often reconsider their position. You have a much bigger problem when you face opposition, the subject of the next chapter.

5

Secret 5—
Move Your Opposition

You gain a lot of power by identifying and understanding your opposition. Unlike skeptics, who can generally be reached through facts, opponents are sometimes unreachable with tools of intellect because they are driven partly or solely by emotion.

If you're a responsive leader, someone will always be unhappy and speaking up to challenge you. Your curiosity about opportunities, active listening, receptivity to questions, and moral compass are all features of your leadership that can provoke opposition. As long as it's healthy opposition—that is, there are facts at the core of it—then you can learn from it, respond to it intelligently, and benefit from it. In contrast, unhealthy opposition is nothing more than an emotional attack.

As a quick exercise, think of people you would consider opponents within your organization, in your community, or even in your own family. These are people who aren't just questioning why you're doing something and are open to engaging in dialogue. Instead, these are people who give you push back—at least occasionally—that is unrelenting. Place them somewhere along this continuum:

Emotion ←————————————————→ Intellect

In this chapter, we'll explore the various types of opposition and how you might move it into positive territory—from emotion-driven challenges to keenly fact-based criticism. As part of this exploration, we want to consider types of people who *choose* to be opponents and, try as you may, you cannot figure out why they are fighting your agenda or point of view. These people are not merely contrarian thinkers, who can be a healthy faction in an organization, but rather people we might describe as

- Manipulators
- Socially/professionally tone-deaf people
- Bullies
- Bigots

At its most useful, opposition is a vital element in the cultivation of responsive leadership. It does a couple of important things. First, it helps you answer the interrogatives related to options and contrarian thinking that had not occurred to you: who else, what else, when else, where else, how else. As a corollary, it helps you refine your message.

When you understand not only what the healthy opposition has to say, but also what is driving the opposition, you are in a position to respond effectively. You can do one of several things to your strategy, such as factoring other arguments into it or adjusting the way you communicate the strategy and its benefits.

In contrast, when you perceive that the opposition is not constructive and/or does not reflect respect for your leadership or even your person, then you are in territory where concepts like firing or resigning come into play.

When I first began my position at Dimock, because I was a new messenger, I had an opportunity to reshape the culture. By virtue of using words such as *new* and *reshape,* I'm implying that I automatically met with some opposition, which came from anyone with both feet planted in the status quo. Considering how desperate the situation there was, however, it was often a relatively smooth process to harmonize the viewpoints of the opposition with strategies of my design.

I tried the same new messenger approach at Wheelock and got a much more mixed response. Whether it was about budgeting, strategic planning, tenure criteria, shared governance, student behavior, admissions decisions—and the list goes on and on—individuals and group within the administration, faculty, and senior staff were not, and could not be, always on the same page. We were challenged by our different understanding and views of what values were at stake—what was the "right" thing do to, what was the fair decision, whether equality or equity should prevail, which of several competing goals should take precedence in fulfilling the college's mission. All of this forced me to rethink how to deal with the opposition.

I'll go into more detail on the Wheelock challenges and the opponents I encountered all along the continuum in this chapter.

INTELLECT-BASED OPPOSITION

A practical example of how I worked with the opposition relates to increasing enrollment at the college.

Wheelock's enrollment was down to a total of about 500 students and, coming from a business background rather than academia, I saw that as a market share problem. With that in mind, at one of the early meetings at Wheelock, I described the students as customers: "They can come and go as they choose. They pay us for services. They can get those services somewhere else. They are our customers and we have to take action to bring them here and retain them."

Many of the faculty members' eyes grew wide—in horror more than curiosity. "They are students!" they cried, not wishing to characterize people paying for their academic expertise as customers. They argued that the service of education is different from a haircut or car wash and we should never think of our students as *just* customers. Even though we had many business professionals on this board of trustees, because they were in the academic environment and steeped in the vocabulary and traditions of higher education, some of them also seemed offended by the label *customer*. But it was primarily the faculty that was intoxicated by the smell of sheepskin and determined that their protégés would never be called customers. To me, this was an opportunity to sober them up.

We advertised the advantages of earning a degree at Wheelock, despite the fact that faculty—opposing me again—wanted to invest those resources in faculty recruitment and salaries. Ultimately, our billboards, sponsorship announcements on the National Public Radio affiliate WBUR, and social media promotion got *Wheelock* to come up more when high schoolers were searching for academic opportunities. Our efforts resulted in a 50 percent rise in enrollment over the course of the next few years.

Thinking of students as customers paid off—for Wheelock and for them. As students came on campus and saw efforts to enhance their campus experience (the new student center) and their ability to be competitive in the job market (the new technology center), they were customers who determined they were getting their money's worth. That level of satisfaction breeds other customers.

Aside from its practical benefits, looking for opposition also has the lofty benefit of helping to keep leaders on the right ethical path. Ethical conduct and questions of integrity, justice, and equity are points of debate in many business environments. Turn an ear to those who question a policy or have issues with a decision; they might have a point worth listening to.

For purely practical reasons, Apple's former CEO John Sculley would have been wise to listen to his opposition instead of driving the Newton project forward. Newton was not Sculley's concept, as iPhone later became Steve Jobs' when he returned to take the helm at the company he cofounded; it was the vision of technology developer Michael Tchao. But Newton became Sculley's baby; he proudly named it a personal digital assistant and broadcast the message that Newton would revolutionize personal computing. In theory, Newton did represent an important departure from the desktop computer, but it was flawed technology. Its key feature—handwriting recognition—did not function well. When it debuted, it also needed several hundred dollars in upgrades just to deliver on promises that it was also a communications device.

Reviews of the product commonly went like this one in the *New York Times:* "Apple promised too much and failed to deliver a useful device."[1] Sculley did not let the critical noise put him off course. He could identify his opposition, but he didn't appear to quite understand that his favorite product faced the force of it. The Newton debacle is just one of those that contributed to Sculley's undoing.

From both insider and outsider accounts, I've concluded that Sculley was a responsive leader in a limited way, but primarily, he typified the systemic leader I described in the Introduction: he came in with a clear idea of what he could do and what he wanted to do. Sculley had earned a great reputation as an innovative marketer during his years as president of PepsiCo, where he led the company in a successful market-sharing grab against Coca-Cola. At Apple, he tried to mass-market the Macintosh computer to cut into his PC rivals' market share. Those strategies are not inherently flawed; however, a systematic leader tends to be less attuned to opposition because he believes he has proven that his way works best. In the face of legitimate, fact-based opposition, such as the kind he encountered with Newton, he once again decided to stay the course.

And again, as I said in the Introduction, a responsive leader aims for a shared vision. It's not about imposing what one individual thinks should happen, but about responding to the genuine needs of the organization and building a vision shared by the people who aim to meet those needs. A responsive leader respects the value of—and responds to—strong, intellect-based opposition.

INTELLECT-BASED OPPOSITION TINGED WITH EMOTION

I would never argue that people who show emotion about a topic or project cannot think. Sometimes their word choice isn't the best, their presentation is over the top, or they corrupt the facts with opinions, but that doesn't necessarily mean *all* their information is incorrect.

A now classic example of this is people in the public health arena who made arguments about how to handle the growing crisis of AIDS in the 1980s. Posters featuring handsome white men promoted the use of condoms to practice safe sex because "many people believed that AIDS was a disease that affected only white gay communities."[2] In 1985, the Black Gay and Lesbian Leadership Forum issued their own poster featuring handsome black men to spread the word that AIDS didn't discriminate based on color so *all* gay men should use condoms.

All of these voices, as well as our community at Dimock—with some of us differing, or even contradicting each other—soon became the opposition to Reagan Administration policies. In 1987, Congress explicitly banned the use of federal funds for AIDS prevention and education. Although Dimock and others in the public health arena were fundamentally in agreement with other factions of society who opposed this federal policy, our messaging was not unified even though our hearts and minds were. Emotions ran very, very high in the face of official language—the law of the land—that prohibited federal funding for AIDS prevention or education campaigns that were perceived to promote or encourage "directly or indirectly, homosexual activities."[3] This was the language of conservative senator Jesse Helms, signed into law by President Ronald Reagan.

Anyone reading this who is old enough to remember that time will likely cringe and feel some of the emotion that we felt at the time. Emotion was part of what kept us going at Dimock, seeking private funding for our groundbreaking programs for AIDS patients, which I describe more in the next chapter. Emotion was part of what fueled momentum in much of the public health movement to protect people of all lifestyles and colors from the ravages of AIDS.

In short, emotion is not an inherently negative element of opposition. It does need to be identified, though. As a leader, part of your job is to ascertain to what extent the emotions of those who oppose you may have affected the quality of the information you are hearing from them.

EMOTION-DRIVEN OPPOSITION

You may recognize that your opposition is driven by emotion—they love something you don't stand for or hate something you do stand for; they desire to see someone like you succeed (man, woman, person of color, homosexual, heterosexual, and others) or desire to see someone like you fail. And the list goes on.

In some cases, the arguments opposing your plan or decision may be laced with evidence that it is flawed. You may encounter an attempt to concoct a believable argument that pushes you back. In other cases, your opponent won't even bother. It's what and who you are that evokes the challenges, not what you think or do.

Emotion Supported by "Fake Facts"

This is the realm of conspiracy theories and coverup stories. People who are driven by emotion in their opposition, but either do not recognize it or are embarrassed by that reality, can go to great lengths to construct narratives that support their point of view. Here are three examples, from politics, industry, and organizational dynamics.

The Birther Movement: Article II of the US Constitution requires that the President of the United States be a natural-born citizen. Former Senator John McCain, who ran for president against Barack Obama in 2008 qualified even though he was born in Panama. He was born to US citizens at the Coco Solo Naval Air Station; his father was a naval officer stationed on this "American soil" in a foreign land. That fact was widely known and widely embraced. In contrast, a huge number of fringe theorists known as *birthers* maintained that Obama was not qualified to be president because he was born in another country—or some version of that—when in fact he was born in Hawaii.

The permutations of the conspiracy theory seemed to be endless. Some birthers argued Obama was born in Kenya, where his father was from. No, others said, he was born in the United States, but he became an Indonesian citizen as a child, so he lost his US citizenship. No, he doesn't qualify because he was born with dual citizenship, both British and American. The theories got so out of control—promoted by billboards, ads, and rallies—that reasonable people wondered if the next wave of accusations would have Barack Obama coming from a distant galaxy.

Whether the root of the opposition was the intense desire to defeat a popular Democrat or the fear or hatred of an African-American becoming president, it was emotion-based. The birther movement persisted even after the pre-election release in 2008 of Obama's Hawaiian birth certificate. And even after a long form of the birth certificate was released in 2011—it's known as a Certificate of Live Birth, and a certified copy of the original was released—a Gallup poll indicated that

13 percent of all Americans and 23 percent of Republicans still doubted Obama's citizenship at birth.[4] And even in 2017, survey results published by *Newsweek* indicated that 57 percent of the people who said they voted for Donald Trump bought into his assertion that Barack Obama was born in Kenya.[5]

The Ethanol Fallacy: The Clean Air Amendments of 1990 forced petroleum refiners to use additives to make gas burn cleaner. The environmental movement had made inroads politically and made air pollution from autos an important element in its legislative agenda. Ethanol was a feel-good additive. It pushed corn prices up, so US farmers reaped financial benefits, and it helped make driving a car less environmentally offensive because it does burn cleaner than gasoline.

That fact soon became a fake fact of the environment movement, however, and it was repeated and sustained almost solely by the corn farmers who were benefitting from it. The emotion driving them was fear that, if too many people found out the truth about ethanol, the farmers would lose their cash cow.

The truth is that gasoline technology has since advanced to the point where gas now burns cleaner without additives. Even former Vice President Al Gore, one of the most high-profile environmentalists in the world, does not support the way the United States enforces ethanol reliance. In 2010, he admitted that "corn-based ethanol in the United States was not a good policy."[6]

Yet years later, many people are still under the impression that it is only opponents of the environment who question the use of ethanol in gasoline. The strength of the initial message—before it became a fake fact—has been enough to sustain its life and arm those opposed to eliminating ethanol use.

Favoritism: A month after the *Deepwater Horizon* oil rig exploded and killed eleven men, Secretary of the Interior Ken Salazar broke up the regulatory agency that had oversight into offshore drilling into three different organizations. Mounting evidence showed that the agency, the Minerals Management Service (MMS), rubberstamped industry requests on many occasions, leading to serious safety violations. At least one of those violations was ultimately linked to the *Deepwater Horizon* tragedy.

The fake fact that surfaced time and again was that the companies operating in the Gulf of Mexico met safety requirements and were in compliance with US government regulations. Because the message came from federal sources who had good credentials and years of experience, virtually no one looked past it. Nonetheless, the driving motivation for a surprising number of officials—nearly one-third of the employees of the significant MMS operation called Royalty in Kind—was that they accepted gifts and bribes in exchange for rubberstamping requests.

The emotion driving them was fear—fear that their affairs with industry people, the free hotel rooms after parties, and the recreational drugs supplied by their company contacts would be discovered.[7]

All Emotion, No Reason

Opposition that is unabashedly emotional, such as opposing a boss because she is female, or relentlessly challenging a supervisor because he is gay is, at the very least, frustrating. It might even be painful if you are on the receiving end. The critical step you must take as soon as you recognize it is this: *Do not take it personally.* We'll look more closely at the importance of this in Chapter 7 on recovering quickly.

In absorbing the challenge or criticism as a personal attack, you put yourself in a downward spiral. You are off your game in many ways—timing, interaction with others, decision-making—because you have diminished your focus on the mission of the organization by putting too much of it on yourself.

Leaders of every stripe encounter this kind of opposition at some point. I know of one leader who came into corporate America after rising to the rank of a three-star general. Some people did not want to work for him because he represented his country's war machine. I know of other leaders who had emotion-driven opposition because they were men or women of color. The bias may be unconscious, but it drives people to find reasons to make you wrong.

People have certain beliefs that shape the way they approach issues and people. Many people aren't even able to identify what some of those beliefs are, and that is the nature of unconscious bias.

I heard a story recently from someone who grew up in a relatively small town in Pennsylvania. She was reconnecting with high school friends with whom she'd had very limited contact over the past forty-five years. Through politically charged email exchanges that certain classmates were circulating, she realized that some of them were very vocal about their support for building a wall between Mexico and the United States. She thought hard about where such a bias would have come from, and then one possibility occurred to her: when they were kids, the rough part of town every-one associated with illegal drugs and murders was where the Hispanic immigrants lived. One of their classmates had gotten into serious trouble because of his association with this violence and drug culture. Could it be, she wondered, that this awful memory from their youth was still infecting their thinking about Hispanic immigrants?

Many of these classmates still lived in or near that home town, whereas she had gone on to live in eight different urban areas, each with a great deal of diversity. If she ever had those biases, they were most likely over-whelmed by the positive experiences she had over the past few decades with people from all over the world.

After all those years, could those people learn to rec-ognize their unconscious biases and modify their behav-ior? Human beings are full of surprises. If you're in a work environment with people affected by such biases, your awareness of what's going on will help you step back, not take it personally, and do what you can to help ensure that it doesn't affect attitudes or output. Remember that it isn't about you, even though you may symbolize what they see as a "problem."

Dr. John Ballard (*Decoding the Workplace*), a professor of management at Mount St. Joseph University in Cincin-nati, Ohio, and a workplace dynamics consultant, offers this insight:

> *With so many of these bias-based behaviors, it's difficult to discern the true nature of the situation. So much of it is hid-den from you. You end up having to work with the anger or meanness, sometimes without having any way of addressing what's causing it.*
>
> *You may be dealing with pure emotion. But part of your job as a leader is to try to ascertain if you are correctly perceiving*

the situation. Ask yourself if there is anything you did—your management style, differences in the way you treat different people—that would invite or add to the problem.[8]

Ballard notes that perceptual issues that inflame opposition can sometimes be addressed, particularly one-on-one, by establishing common ground. Military men and women in battle realize acutely that their common ground is an enemy who wishes to kill them, regardless of their color, religion, gender, or where they were born. In a work environment, identifying a common enemy or a strategy about which there is a shared passion can sometimes move people together. Doing this sounds simple, but some leaders impose their perception of who the enemy is or what the cause is on others instead of listening to them to find out what their priorities are.

Unfortunately, when the conflict comes down to pure prejudice, then staying or going all comes down to job performance, according to Ballard. If the job gets done well, then life can go on for a while. At some point, however, the conflict is bound to affect other people in the environment, so someone will have to leave.

Toward the end of my time as president of Wheelock College, I encountered what often seemed like senseless opposition from the board. Since then, I've reflected on it, but I think that John Ballard analyzed the problem well during our conversation. Without even knowing the specific circumstances of my situation, he addressed the issue of a senior leader finding the tide of board opinion pushing against her instead of moving with her.

Having gone from the Air Force into academia, Ballard had encountered many examples of people—even leaders—being part of the "out" group. Try as they might, they would never be part of the "in" group. They didn't have multiple generations of relatives who attended a prestigious military academy, or they did not have academic credentials from an Ivy League school. He mentioned that he even noticed unintentional exclusion of one of his colleagues of color from certain things. It wasn't as though people thought he was less competent; they just didn't think to include him. The Law of Attraction can therefore work in ways we don't even realize: even unconsciously, we can be drawn to certain people just because they look like us and we can walk away from relationships with those who do not.

Ballard has concluded the following when it comes to a senior leader who was first accepted by the "in" group and was then was shut out over time:

> *Usually, in those cases, it's not a function of something they do, but something the "in" group does. There's a change of perception on the part of the "in" group, with the likely issue being a change in the composition of the "in" group.*[9]

This is an apt and objective description of one thing that ultimately worked against me at Wheelock. I will go into that a bit more toward the end of the book to share signs and signals of such a shift. One thing to note here is that a responsive leader may be so focused on her team and the success of their projects and programs, that she might miss the indicators of a change in the power structure that could affect her job security. In other words, a responsive leader is not necessarily politically astute.

Ballard has observed some leaders successfully changing the board to be composed of more people in their image, thus actually changing the nature of the "in" group. Whether or not this is achievable may well relate to where the leader is in her life cycle as senior executive. It's another Goldilocks kind of conundrum: not too soon, not too late, but when the time is perfectly right. That perfectly right time would likely be when she is riding highest on success and is not having any serious opposition.

THE LOST CAUSES

Let's consider the opponents you will probably have to fire or cause to resign. And unfortunately, if they are in the power structure, you are the one who probably needs to walk away from them and move to a different environment. These are the

- Manipulators

- Socially/professionally tone-deaf people

- Bullies

- Bigots

Manipulators

In their book, *Get People to Do What You Want*, former military interrogator Gregory Hartley and human behavior expert Maryann Karinch use Maslow's hierarchy of needs as a threshold concept in teaching people how human beings are manipulated. Looking at the hierarchy from the bottom up, we see that people first try to ensure their survival needs are met. After that, they are most concerned about their safety. Having addressed those fundamental needs that relate to staying alive, they want connection to other beings. The psychological need that sits above this is a desire for accomplishment, a sense that others appreciate them for their contributions. At the top of the hierarchy is self-actualization. At this level, people feel as though they have achieved their potential. They have a truly satisfying life.

Predators, as well as *benevolent manipulators* such as an Army drill sergeant, know that fear is a strong motivator. If you can arouse fear in a person—that he or she will lose something precious and be pushed to a lower level of the hierarchy—then you have power to influence that person's behavior. Conversely, if you see someone's intense desire to rise to the next level, and you have the ability to help make that happen, then you also have power to manipulate that individual.

Socially/Professionally Tone-Deaf People

Does this sound familiar? You try to have reasonable conversations with some people and you walk away unsatisfied and, perhaps, angry at the impasse that always seems to characterize such attempts. They twist your words, take a sharp deviation in logic, or seem confused at what you're saying, even if it's as simple as "We have a staff meeting at two o'clock in the Blue Room."

One of my friends was director of communications at an organization and inherited an employee like this. She went to her boss, the president of the company, and her boss gave her the budget for outplacement counseling for the employee. It was an elegant and practical solution that a lot of leaders do not pursue because they want to "fix the problem" in house. My friend recognized that her situation could not be fixed; this was the wrong environment for this person—she just didn't know why.

The nature of the job provoked contentious behavior that bordered on sociopathy. The outplacement counselor determined that the employee, hired to assist with event planning and public relations, really wanted to be a photographer. The counselor helped guide her toward the marketing department of a company where she could apply her photography skills.

Bullies

The University of Cincinnati posts online an overview of its graduate program in Behavior Analysis: Understanding Bullying Behavior. The answer to "What Is Bullying?" is helpful to anyone in a work environment, at any level, who feels threatened:

> *Bullying is defined as negative behavior designed to hurt others either physically or emotionally. A bully assumes a position of power over a victim or victims, either using physical size or a dominant social status. Bullying is usually an ongoing situation that involves cruelty toward a target. Sometimes, people confuse fighting with bullying. The difference between fighting and bullying is the balance of power: When engaged in fighting, students have equal positions of power, but when bullying is occurring, an imbalance of power is present.*[10]

A responsive leader keeps an open door, but that practice can leave you vulnerable to people who exploit your receptivity. If you don't keep good notes, you may not realize—expect emotionally—that someone on your staff or your board is bullying you. In Appendix C, I outline a system of notetaking that will support your analysis of opposition, and it's particularly helpful when that opposition might be classified as bullying or bigoted. In brief, the system of note-taking involves people, places, things, and time—the four areas of discovery/disclosure that I introduced in Chapter 1. Using these four areas to organize your notes is part of a system that many intelligence officers use to keep input well-structured when they are interrogating someone.

Bigots

These are verbal and/or emotional abusers who find who or what you are offensive to them. The same advice on notetaking that applies to bullies applies to bigots. It is essential that you (a) not take their comments and actions personally and (b) document every encounter in a methodical way. The approach described in Appendix C will help you organize your information that will be useful later.

MANAGING HEALTHY OPPOSITION

"You once encouraged me to express my opinion if I had anything relevant to say." This is how the character known as Seven of Nine on *Star Trek: Voyager* begins her opposition to a decision made by Captain Kathryn Janeway. When Janeway provides her reasoning for sticking to her course of action, Seven of Nine counters, "Then we are in disagreement."

Janeway ends the episode with a sentiment with which I wholeheartedly concur: "I dread the day when everyone on this ship agrees with me."[11]

As a responsive leader, you invite questions and opinions that keep you on your toes. You manage challenges to your decisions by keeping yourself and the people around you focused on the shared vision for the organization. Managing healthy opposition within your organization means, first, seeing how the source of it perceives that opposition as serving that shared vision. Once you're clear on that, you can hopefully have a constructive conversation on next steps. When the opposition is coming from more than one voice, it might be time to use some tried-and-true techniques to coordinate thinking within a group.

At a difficult time at Wheelock, we had a consultant named Joanne come in. In one of our retreats, she drew two lines on the board. A red line about twelve inches from the bottom of the board and a green line about twenty-five inches above the red line. She told us our job was to stay in the green. She challenged us that every time we sunk to the red, we had to rebound and move into the green.

Our job as leaders is to stay in the green so our organization can stay in the green. As I said in the Introduction, start by leading yourself.

If you're in the red, you're in a stop zone. You cannot bring the organization up to the green if you are sitting in the red, so do some self-examination to figure out what you are doing to contribute to your own failure. Start by asking yourself questions related to the 7 Secrets in this book:

- How are you seeking new opportunities?

- What are you doing that demonstrates you are leading from the heart?

- How ready are you to move on if your values are compromised or if circumstances or people make it impossible for you to function optimally?

- How well are you staying on point with your messages?

- When people question your decisions, how effective and mission-focused is your response?

- How do you demonstrate your loyalty to your team?

- What in your behavior reminds you and others that you are resilient?

Working to stay in the green sounds incredibly simplistic, but if you're in a room with people who feel demoralized and/or contentious, just hearing something simple that makes sense and creates a common focus can be a catalytic moment. The concept of staying in the green gets people thinking about unifying with a common objective in mind. No matter where they are coming from or what they oppose, if they are committed to helping the organization, if not the leader, stay in the green, then opposition might be channeled for good ends.

Another way of approaching the opposition is ascertaining what the opposing argument represents in terms of the organization's risk tolerance. Jim McCormick (*The Power of Risk*), who has researched the nature and role of risk-taking in organizations for decades, coaches C-level business executives in the power of intelligent risk-taking.[12] He has found that there are generally three places where risk takers are found in an organization and one of them is at the top. One of the reasons they are at the top is that they have proven their ability to identify and implement risks effectively. Another place where you find them is on their way to the top because they have the ability to do the same as the top-tier risk takers and the organization recognizes that as a valuable trait. A leader sometimes gets opposition from those individuals because they have a risk tolerance that's higher than the leader's and/or higher than the organization's. The third place is on their way out the door because they are discouraged from taking risks. They get frustrated and pursue a new environment where they are encouraged to dive into the deep end of the pool.

On the reverse end of the spectrum in terms of opposition—and this is probably more common—the leader is challenged by someone or some group that thinks her proposal is *too* risky. People with a relatively low risk tolerance are a vital force within an organization because they voice concerns that the leader may have underrated or missed entirely. They are not the ones who propel the organization forward at a fast pace, but they are often the ones who help make sure that the risks taken are intelligent ones rather than outrageous ones. My proposal to build a new student center at Wheelock received opposition from this faction on campus and on the board.

A responsive leader recognizes that both the more-risk and less-risk opponents can help refine his implementation process related to the risk. In the case of the student center, the path to doing that was first getting a firm determination that we could build on the site. The second was finding seed money outside of the college budget to begin planning efforts. The third was attracting the talent needed to design a noteworthy building that represented the college's future.

Finally, general guidance on reading and managing opposition involves

Active listening: Your ears play an important role in listening, but so do your eyes. Pay attention to both the verbal and nonverbal input you are receiving. Sometimes, you may look at a person's face and read anxiety, even though the words coming out of his mouth project confidence.

Knowing your triggers: Words and actions may set you off and you must know what they are. I know someone who found himself getting tense and defensive when someone came into his personal space—defined by him as about two feet. Until he brought that reality forward in his consciousness, an innocent slap on the shoulder made him feel as though the other person was on the offensive.

Staying alert to signs that opposition represents a serious disease: Psychiatrist Elisabeth Kübler-Ross is most known for her five stages of dying: denial, anger, bargaining, depression, and acceptance. They are useful for a leader to know because the same experiences can describe a career, or an entire organization, in a death spiral. I explore this in some depth in Chapter 7, but here, suffice it to say that opposition can trigger this spiral—but it need not end badly if you stay alert, looking for the signs.

You cannot lead well, and you are not leading well, without opposition. Your task is to determine when it is healthy in order to respond to it for the good of your organization, and when it is unhealthy in order to quash it. Your other option is to leave it behind and find a new environment in which your leadership can thrive. That is one of the key topics covered in Chapters 7 and 8.

6

Secret 6—
Value the Interconnectedness
of People

L eaders are often challenged by board members, employees, or constituents to fire, disregard, or otherwise abandon a person or group because they represent inconvenience. For one my colleagues, it was an ostensibly simple matter of someone alerting her to the fact that an extremely overweight, but highly qualified candidate had been passed over for a promotion, while an attractive, less-qualified individual had gotten the job. This simple matter turned into an Equal Employment Opportunity Commission lawsuit in which the overweight employee won a large settlement.

That's a straightforward example of honoring the value of a person and putting backbone into that expression. Leaders experience many, subtler challenges on a daily basis, however. The essence of these challenges is wrapped up in the temptation to be selfish—we want to grab the accolades, control the process, dominate the agenda, and so on. Many Americans label such actions as good old-fashioned competitive spirit. Absolutely nothing is wrong with competitive spirit, but regardless of what other people might suggest, business is not a boxing match. A company can win, and win big, when its people recognize their interconnectedness and go to battle *together*.

REWARDS OF INTERCONNECTEDNESS

Let's begin by looking at the rewards of genuine collaboration. First, we will take a humanistic approach. Then, we will consider research and compelling corporate stories that illustrate the revenue and innovation results—the quantifiable success measures—of interconnectedness.

Relying on Ubuntu

One day, a western anthropologist went to Africa to study the social behavior of an indigenous tribe. He proposed a game to the children and they willingly agreed to be part of it. He put a basket filled with fruits underneath a tree and told the children that whoever would reach the basket first would win the whole basket and could eat the fruits all by him or herself.

He lined them all up and raised his hand to give the start signal. Ready. Set. Go!

The children took each other's hands and started running together. They all reached the basket at the same time. Then they sat down in a big circle and enjoyed the fruits together, laughing and smiling all the time.

The anthropologist could not believe what he saw and he asked them why they had waited for each other as one could have taken the whole basket all for him- or herself.

The children shook their heads and replied, "Ubuntu, how can one of us be happy if all the others are sad?"[1]

Ubuntu is a concept described by Archbishop Emeritus Desmond Tutu as

> *. . . the essence of being human. Ubuntu speaks particularly about the fact that you can't exist as a human being in isolation. It speaks about our interconnectedness. You can't be human all by yourself, and when you have this quality— Ubuntu—you are known for your generosity.*[2]

Archbishop Tutu brought the message of Ubuntu to us in person at Wheelock. We had awarded him an honorary degree and invited him to campus. What he gave Wheelock and our community at large was far more than we could have ever expected. He was our featured speaker at a three-day youth symposium that drew about 500 middle and high school students and another 150 adults who were their teachers and counselors from the area to the Wheelock campus. They were from public, private, and charter schools—a diverse group of young people and adults— who came together to discuss violence and forgiveness.

Archbishop Tutu told us some memorable stories from his experiences on the Truth and Reconciliation Commission. The Commission was formed in 1995, the year after Nelson Mandela took office, to look into all apartheid-related crimes in South Africa. It carried the objective of providing an official process for mending racial disparities. One particularly memorable story he told us involved a question a fourteen-year-old girl posed to the Commission. She had lost her entire family—mother, father, brothers, and sisters—to police brutality. Standing before the Commissioners, she said she didn't know exactly who had perpetrated the murderous acts: "Who do I forgive?"

Let's consider how an answer to a question like this applies in any environment, even a corporate one. For example, let's say layoffs are occurring in your company and your entire department is gutted. The brutality the South African girl experienced is not present, but the situation still engenders pain, resentment, and anger. You don't even want to show up for work anymore because your team is gone. "Who do you forgive?" is a question you would probably link to "Whose bright idea was it to let all these people go instead of finding another solution?" The CEO? Shareholders? The board of directors?

In such a case, your challenge is not necessarily to forgive individual people, but to forgive the people who sustain a system or practices that result in the hurt you experienced.

Forgiveness doesn't mean you are giving in. It doesn't mean you are pardoning or excusing a person or group because you think what they did was right or justifiable on any level. In forgiving, you also don't have to announce to the world that you've forgiven a person or a group. And when you forgive someone, you don't give up the privilege, or perhaps the need, to feel angry or resentful. It does not make everything okay or mean that whatever awful thing happened is forgotten. Finally, forgiveness is about you, not about whoever hurt you.

Who should that young woman have forgiven? The people who were misguided and hateful enough to kill her family—not just the people who actually did it, but anyone who shared their prejudice and would have carried out the same heinous acts. Forgiving them would likely have given her more clarity about how wrong they were. Forgiveness is a tool that can help move a person along, step by step, to face reality and achieving a sense of resolution.

At the Wheelock youth symposium, a young man from the inner city—a euphemism for a teenager whose family is struggling financially and is surrounded by violence—asked the Archbishop: "How do you forgive someone who's been bad to you?" As I recall, the Archbishop said to him, "You don't have to like these people, but you do have to love them." And that is when he explored the concept of Ubuntu with the people participating in the symposium. In this context, *love* meant—and I'm translating here—a sincere appreciation for our interconnectedness as human beings and a way of behaving that reflects that appreciation.

Sir Richard Branson values the Ubuntu concept so much that his Virgin.com website discusses "How the Ubuntu philosophy can have a positive impact on your business."[3] One of the points made on the site is that Ubuntu cultivates a sense of accountability. And who would question that accountability is an element that is good for business? If, in fact, you conduct business in a way that displays how much you value the interconnectedness of human beings, then you are taking responsibility to lift them up with you. Like the kids with the anthropologist in the earlier story, you will all make an effort to capture the basket of fruit together.

Leaders may be driven by both emotion and intellect when they strive to demonstrate that they value their staff, board, clients, and others around them. As with any of the 7 Secrets, however, it's vital that emotion not overtake the process—even in personnel challenges. Similarly, it's important to remember the merits of bringing positive emotions into the decision-making process. As humans, when we achieve a balance between emotion and intellect, it helps keep our leadership healthy.

Stated another way, creating and implementing policies and practices that engender interconnectedness involve planning as well as caring.

Profiting from Interconnectedness

If you have to choose between hiring only super-smart people who are good solo operators and hard-working people of average intelligence and good team spirit, which do you choose? If you're like a lot of leaders—particularly in highly competitive industries such as technology and medical research—you may choose the former. However, research done by William Muir at Purdue University and a research team at the Massachusetts Institute of Technology (MIT) might make you think twice about that choice.

Muir is a professor of Animal Sciences at Purdue and he undertook an experiment in chicken evolution in the 1990s. He goal was to increase egg-laying productivity in hens. He put groups of nine hens in each cage and then, in brief, he selected the most productive hen from each cage to breed the next generation of hens. In theory, if the capacity for egg-laying was an inherited trait, his process should have produced a strain of superior egg layers. That did not happen. Instead, the experiment resulted in a strain of extremely aggressive hens, only three of which survived because they pecked the others to death. Needless to say, egg productivity declined.

At the same time Muir was breeding his super chickens, he had a parallel experiment going on. He chose *all* the hens from the cage of hens that had produced the best collectively to breed another generation of hens and he continued this practice for several generations. As a result, egg productivity increased 160 percent in only a few generations, "an almost unheard-of response to artificial selection in animal breeding experiments."[4]

At least two lessons emerge from Muir's research. One is that creating a society—or a company—by selecting *only* the best performers ratchets up the competitive impulse to a destructive level. Another is that productivity of a group is not just a matter of what one individual does; the social environment where that individual operates is a major factor.

Moving from hens to humans, consider how a bit of MIT research is a good companion to Muir's experiments. Hundreds of volunteers, some with exceptionally high IQs, were grouped into teams and given very hard problems to solve. The teams that excelled were neither those who had one or two geniuses on them nor those that had the highest aggregate IQ. Those that rose to the top had specific characteristics, which Margaret Heffernan, entrepreneur and former CEO of five businesses, described in her TED Talk, "Forget the pecking order at work."

> *First of all, they showed high degrees of social sensitivity to each other. This is measured by something called the Reading the Mind in the Eyes Test. It's broadly considered a test for empathy, and the groups that scored highly on this did better. Secondly, the successful groups gave roughly equal time to each other, so that no one voice dominated, but neither were there any passengers. . . The striking thing about this experiment is that it showed what we know, which is some groups do better than others, but what's key to that is their social connectedness to each other.[5]*

The MIT example is part of Heffernan's compelling case for the monetary and innovative value of building *social capital,* a term used by sociologists. It came out of their studies of communities that displayed remarkable resilience under duress. She says,

> *Social capital is the reliance and interdependency that builds trust.*
>
> *. . .Social capital is what gives companies momentum, and social capital is what makes companies robust. What does*

this mean in practical terms? It means that time is every-thing, because social capital compounds with time. So teams that work together longer get better, because it takes time to develop the trust you need for real candor and openness. And time is what builds value.[6]

Cultivating social capital is standard operating procedure for a responsive leader. To some extent, it also reflects a long-admired Aristotelian tenet that "the whole is greater than the sum of its parts."

THE MORAL IMPERATIVE TO CONNECT

Early in my experience at Dimock, the most challenging healthcare issue we faced was both patients from the community and some of their caregivers at Dimock suffering from AIDS. In the early days of the epidemic—I started at the center in 1983—Dimock had staff members who were taking care of AIDS patients, getting sick, and dying themselves. The first major article about the disease had come out less than two years before in the *New York Times* ("Rare Cancer Seen in 41 Homosexuals"), so awareness of the disease and how it was transmitted was low. The word *AIDS* had not even entered the vocabulary when Dimock staff began taking care of infected patients!

Some of our staff were so deeply engaged in caring for patients that they were going to funerals almost every week. They were relentless in their devotion to treating and comforting the sick and dying.

But it was the presence of AIDS within our staff that created urgency in the organization. The death of two of our most prominent caregivers helped all of us at Dimock quickly coalesce our commitment to strengthening our AIDS-related services. It was this sobering time for the Dimock community that helped us form a policy around the disease and how we officially treated our own people who were sick.

I was on board immediately with creating a policy but saw that this would not be an easy battle to win. The popular mentality was that "other people, careless people, people not like us" get AIDS.

In our situation, though, the AIDS sufferers on our staff were not other people—they were colleagues. They were not careless, they were caring. And, yes, they were like us. They were exactly like us.

As the brand-new head of this organization, the leadership requirement for me was, paradoxically, both very simple and highly complex. It was a "do the right thing" moment on one hand; on the other, it was the real challenge of doing the right thing and potentially alienating some of the people we needed most to survive, that is, big donors and key board members.

I was already dealing with an organization that was financially stricken and experiencing reputational loss. I had to ask myself this: How will I lead us to take a stand to support the good people who are the soul of the organization and, at the same time, not shock supporters who see AIDS as a product of an aberrant lifestyle?

Part of what leaders do is have the courage to say to their team, "I will stand by you. No matter what." In our case, the result was a policy that set precedents among organizations with employees who had AIDS. We made sure they remained integrated in the community; they received care and retained their dignity and their jobs.

THE PRACTICAL IMPERATIVE TO CONNECT

After Harvey Weinstein's sexual harassment scandal drove the company he helped found into Chapter 11 bankruptcy, companies throughout the United States were forced to recognize the financial implications of the #MeToo movement. They now had a practical imperative to connect all their employees through gender awareness training. In the most punitive terms, the training could have the effect of interrupting connections if it became a lecture of "don't do this; don't do that." However, if presented in the most positive way, this training is about respecting the rights and sensitivities of all coworkers. It's an exercise in improving empathy, of walking in another's shoes.

Since the incident with Weinstein, and the rash of other corporate rude awakenings that followed, an esti-mated 52 percent of US companies have reviewed and, in many cases, revised their sexual harassment policies, according to the career consulting firm of Challenger, Gray & Christmas.[7] These companies were forced to do something to connect employees in a healthier way, to help them collaborate with greater respect for each other, partially because the financial implications of not taking this action could have killed them. The estimated cost-per-settlement related to sexual harassment cases is between $75,000 and $125,000, with the highest amount awarded at $168 million as of this writing.[8]

One way that the issue of gender can promote inter-connectedness in the workplace involves people with common interests or characteristics bonding—not to sep-arate themselves from people who aren't like them, but rather to help themselves integrate more effectively into the greater corporate community.

In her bestseller, *Lean In,* and through the Lean In Foundation, Facebook COO Sheryl Sandberg encourages women to help each other assume leadership roles. By joining Lean In Communities, working women are forming their own clubs. There are important things to note about this phenomenon:

- No matter how many benefits there are to being in this group, it still won't get you into the "men's club." (Not that a woman would necessarily want that.) That's not the point, of course. The point is to provide an organizational safe haven for mentoring and bonding.

- Membership in a club like this can be part of a healthy approach to equity in the workplace. If you are in the company of people who care about you and want to protect you, then you have more metaphorical eyes and ears than the ones in your own head. Those eyes and ears can help you recognize opportunities to lead, to take greater risks in your career—to not pigeonhole yourself by being guided by negative thoughts such as "I can't do this because I'm a _____ (woman, person of color, immigrant, and so on)."

In short, a very strong practical reason for a company to promote interconnectedness is a financial one. It is a path to greater earnings when people work harmoniously with one another and a path to reduced costs related to work stoppages (for example, due to a strike or walk out), lawsuits, and mistakes related to the distraction of not getting along with coworkers.

DIVERSITY AND CONNECTION

Earlier, I tried to paint a picture of how recognizing differences as well as similarities can lead to greater unity. However, we also need to concede that underrepresentation of minorities can diminish the chances of that greater unity happening.

If you look around your workplace and don't see anyone like you, it would be normal to feel at least a little isolated. Humans naturally want to feel accepted—bonded—to each other, and the easiest bonds tend to be forged with those with whom we have something in common. When you are the only autistic person in a company of 250 people, or the only woman on a team of 20, or the only person of color in a department of 40 people, then interconnectedness could be an elusive concept—at least in the beginning.

I compiled some statistics related to this for a 2017 speech called "Women as Stakeholders in Higher Education" that I delivered at Boston College at the University Ethics Conference they were hosting. They illustrated for my fellow female university presidents what a bunch of outliers we still were.

- The centuries-long history of scholarship and teaching and learning at higher education institutions has been shaped by men. Older, elite men taught younger elite men—who shared their same background and experiences—how to proceed and succeed in organizing society and its institutions according to their values.

Non-elite men and women, with their different experiences and, to some extent, values, were excluded from education and the higher Socratic discussions.

- More recently, in the 1950s, the profile of the typical campus leader was white, male, married with a family, typically with a doctorate in education. Today, despite a demographic sea change in undergraduate diversity in terms of gender, race, ethnicity, and family background, that leadership profile remains the same.

- Although women have made progress in higher education teaching and have increased their share of college presidencies by one percentage point every two years since the 80s, female senior leaders in higher education lag far behind their male counterparts. Although women are 51 percent of the general population in the United States (roughly 50 percent worldwide) and 56 percent of the student body on US university and college campuses, women still hold only 26 percent of presidencies. At the current slow growth rate of one percent, it will take until approximately 2065 before women hold half of college presidencies, arguably an equal share of campus leadership.

- For women of color, leadership numbers are even more regressive and telling: only 4 percent of college presidents are women of color. Faculty positions such as department heads and provosts on the track to campus leadership are held by only 4 percent of women of color at bachelor's institutions and 8 percent at public master's institutions.

The women in the room where I delivered those numbers needed each other—they needed to feel bonded to each other. We had to take a spirit of interconnectedness back to our institutions of higher learning and look for ways to bring it alive on our campuses. Did that mean that, as part of our leadership, we overtly spearheaded efforts to get greater diversity into our faculty and student populations? Absolutely. We had both the faith and the good sense to know that our success in that effort would lay the foundation for greater emotional and psychological health on our campuses. It's true of a workforce as well.

I was disheartened to learn that men on Wall Street have openly admitted that they are disinclined to hire women due to the #MeToo movement. According to a Bloomberg headline on December 3, 2018: "Wall Street Rule for the #MeToo Era: Avoid Women at All Cost."

Now, more than a year into the #MeToo movement—with its devastating revelations of harassment and abuse in Hollywood, Silicon Valley and beyond—Wall Street risks becoming more of a boy's club, rather than less of one.

. . . While the new personal codes for dealing with #MeToo have only just begun to ripple, the shift is already palpable, according to the people interviewed, who declined to be named. They work for hedge funds, law firms, banks, private equity firms and investment-management firms.[9]

Resurrecting men's clubs in the workplace—or any other group designed specifically to shut out non-members from opportunities and professional respect—is not a responsive leader's answer to disruptions in international communication. Pursuit of diversity is a sound leadership practice. It only works, however, when you remain curious about people who are different from you, when you are open to what they have to offer that you can't possibly feel or know deeply, when you are empathetic so their concerns are not brushed aside, and when you are resilient—because you will get pushback from somebody. You can count on that!

DISCONNECTING WITH DIGNITY

Standing by good people no matter what can also mean that you help them move on. In other words, your concern for both the person and the organization may lead you to fire someone. That person may be aligned with the mission and may even be your friend—this was a situation I once faced—but leaders cannot afford to be narrow-minded about the ways that loyalty can surface in a relationship. When I fired my friend, she remained a friend, but I was able to replace her with someone who was better suited for the position. Her maturity and my approach to the dilemma combined to create a parting that displayed mutual respect.

By bringing the Big 4 to your firing strategy, you can do your part to ensure that the employee you are terminating has a dignified exit. Keep in mind, however, that no matter how you do it, your action could be subconsciously (or consciously) perceived as taking them down a notch on Maslow's hierarchy. The feeling of going from a position of distinction and even power to a situation in which a person feels disgraced and disconnected is potentially devastating. That individual goes from sitting toward the top of the hierarchy to landing near the bottom. It would be normal for them to feel desperate and angry. Here is how the Big 4 can help:

Curiosity: Make sure all your questions about the "why" of the firing have been answered thoroughly. Assertions of an employee's incompetence, insubordination, harassment, or any other category need to be backed with four-part documentation:

> **Time:** When did events or examples occur?

> **People:** Who did the events or examples involve? Who is providing the documentation to you? Sometimes the source of incrimination information is driven by an agenda that may not be obvious, so always question the source.

> **Place:** Did the events or examples occur on site? At a customer location? In a restaurant?

> **Things:** Exactly what happened, or didn't happen?

Humility: Get feedback from people you trust. Firing may be your decision alone, but it will affect others. Try to ascertain what kind of emotional and rational responses this person's coworkers will have to the termination.

Empathy: Just ask yourself how you would want to be treated in this situation. The Golden Rule should flavor your leadership in all situations, but you want to move it to the forefront of your consciousness when you have to terminate someone.

Resilience: As a thinking and feeling person, you may find terminating someone challenging. Although sensitivity keeps you from being abrupt and harsh, it can distract you if you overdose on it. Keep in mind that you are firing someone because you have at least one solid reason to do it. Your action is motivated by your desire for the organization to thrive. You wouldn't be a good leader if you refused to take it.

Termination of an employee should not cut into the connections felt by those who are left.

CONNECTING FEARLESSLY

Throughout tragic literature, we see stories of leaders brought down because they failed to do one or more of these three things:

- Surround themselves with competent, wise people.

- Listen to those competent, wise people.

- Make a concerted effort to understand what they were being told by those people.

A classic tale of all three mistakes converging is Shakespeare's story of King Lear, who allowed the flattery of his two evil daughters to turn him away from the loyal and capable Earl of Kent and his loving daughter, Cordelia. He also doesn't quite understand the wisdom and warnings his Fool imparts.

Humility is the trait that drives your curiosity about whom to bring on board; it is what sustains your ability to listen to capable people so that your ego does not undermine your good judgment.

Surround Yourself with the Best

Bring in people who have strengths that you don't, then acknowledge their triumphs and gifts unequivocally. Don't claim credit for what they did; they are already making you look better than you would have without them.

My father-in-law said to his children, "Find the best advice you can and then. . . follow it." I take this advice to the heart of my leadership. I aim to surround myself with people who are the very best at what they do and then trust them to do their jobs. Inherent in that model is that I will support them with the resources they require to exhibit their excellence.

I'm not great at finance and readily admit that. What kind of wisdom would I exhibit if I hired people who knew less than I did in this area? It's the same with other areas of organizational need. Don't hire people who do not surprise you with their brilliance! Part of this scenario is hiring the best people for the job. To some extent, that comes down to asking questions in the job interview that give you the insights *you* need—not what someone in HR needs, someone who's just focused on whether a person can technically do the job, but what *you* need. Figure out for yourself if the candidate belongs on your team.

Wendy Lea, CEO of Cintrifuse, has developed some provocative interview questions. These help her clients determine their interviewees' expertise as well as the probability of their fitting in with clients—the leaders— and their organizations. A question that potentially covers both is this: "What will I only know about you after we've worked together for a year?"[10] An answer to a question like this tells you nothing substantive, which tells you a lot in terms of whether or not you want this person around you. For instance, consider this response: "Um, you probably wouldn't know I have a tattoo on my arm because I keep it covered up most of the time." In contrast, you would probably find a response like this insightful: "Even though I try to respond promptly, when it comes to big decisions, I prefer to sleep on them. That's not something people usually notice right away."

Forbes contributor Jason Nazar came up with a number of questions that may help you discern if a person with great credentials and demonstrated skills is a person you want beside you every day. Here are ten, slightly paraphrased questions from one of his articles[11]:

- What are you pretending not to know?

- What are your values and are you being true to them?

- If you achieved all of your life's goals, how would you feel?

- What is the most important thing you've learned today?

- What is the one thing you want to get done today?

- If you weren't scared, what would you do?

- What can you do to improve?

- If we could wave a magic wand and do anything together, what would the result look like?

- How do your role models behave?

- What do you think you could help me with if you were my mentor?

When you ask questions such as these, you aren't looking for a "perfect" answer, that is, an answer that's likely to impress anyone who asked the question. You want an answer that gives you insights that are important to you and your organization. If the candidate looks around your office when you ask the mentoring question and says, "I'd coach you in organizing your office," you may not want to hear it, but it does reflect a specific need you have.

Listen to Those Good People

Alison Davis, founder of Davis & Company, specializes in strategic internal communications and this is her succinct observation: "CEOs get their jobs because they're smart, driven and decisive. But they keep their jobs by being smart enough to realize that they don't know everything."[12] In other words, listening to people who have great ideas for solving a problem, skills to get a project done with excellence, and vision for exploiting an opportunity should be part of a CEO's job description. That kind of listening is inextricably linked to job security for a CEO.

Writing for *Forbes*, Mike Myatt, chairman of N2Growth, cautions:

> *Don't be fooled into thinking that being heard is more important than hearing. The first rule in communication is to seek understanding before seeking to be understood. Communication is not a one-way street. I've interviewed and worked with some of the most noted leaders of our time, and to the one, they never miss an opportunity to listen. In fact, they aggressively seek out new and better ways to listen.*[13]

Myatt's tips for becoming a better listener include those we've already covered in notes about active listening—namely, listen with your whole body and pay attention to nonverbal communication. In addition, he also advises that leaders consider things like this:

- *It's not about you.* You will create noise in your head that blocks listening if you are focused on figuring out what you are going to say instead of listening to what the other person has to say.

- *You should never be too busy to listen.* It is true that some people will invariably take advantage of a split second of silence to insert a few words. This tip is not about creating dead air so that people can aimlessly fill it. It's about being responsive rather than dismissive when someone asks—as they say in the military—to speak freely.

- *Recognize the contributions of others.* Even if you are not able to use the input you've received, saying thank you for a thoughtful attempt to contribute establishes an open channel of communication. It demonstrates that you value listening and intend to do it again.

Make Sure You Understand What Was Said

Even though King Lear's Fool is one of the wisest characters in the entire drama, Lear largely disregards or doesn't understand what he has to say. As a result, Lear doesn't heed advice that would have saved him from a wretched end.

A corporate analogy might be Eastman Kodak. Senior leadership kept channeling resources and planning efforts into photographic film products, seemingly not able to interpret the wisdom of advisors who pointed to emerging companies and technologies in the mid-1970s. They probably said, "Look over there! It's a new company called Microsoft. Oh, and over there you can see that IBM is introducing barcode scanners. And look at that: Commodore and Atari are putting computers into people's houses!" Pointing to the proliferation of companies getting consumers oriented toward digital technology made as much impact as the Fool warning Lear about his evil daughters.

When it comes to advice, consider the source. If the source is someone who has given you solid intelligence and insights in the past, then give the next batch of advice from that person more than cursory consideration. Try to ensure you don't overlook something important.

Reconsider the early message and stories about Ubuntu in this chapter. I want to leave you with two related stories to drive home the point that Ubuntu seems to come easily to young, open minds, but the older we get, the more we tend to treat it as an unnecessary and even detrimental concept to thriving.

After Archbishop Tutu conducted the symposium at Wheelock, we launched an annual Ubuntu art exhibit featuring young people's representation of the concept in visual arts and crafts. These led to mature conversations about immigration and other social justice issues as well as the practical benefits in business, education, and elsewhere of connecting with people who are different in some way. After five years of displaying the art in a gallery at Wheelock, our exhibitors were invited to have their work displayed at the Massachusetts State House. After this invitation, the art would first hang at Wheelock for a week, and then it would move to the State House for a week or two.

One of my colleagues helped organize a similar exhibit involving children's art from countries around the world. One of the exhibits featured Cypriot children's art. Despite the children's visual representations of harmony, the gala event attended by adults illustrated the reality of their world: attendees associated with Greek culture and politics socialized on one side of the room while attendees associated with Turkish culture and politics socialized on the other. They gathered to celebrate art depicting a concept they could not grasp.

As a leader, you will see this kind of division in big and small ways. People talk a great game of unity in a product launch or project meetings, and then the "togetherness" degrades into departmental spats and turf wars. The division undermines everything you are trying to do to build organizational strength and success. You need to have Ubuntu live in your organization to reach the highest highs.

7

Secret 7—
Recover Quickly

Great leaders have the ability to recover quickly. Failure is a natural part of risk-taking. The 2017 baseball season saw record-high home runs—but it also saw record-high strikeouts. When you swing hard, sometimes you hit it out of the park, and sometimes you miss the ball entirely, but if you never swing hard, you don't have a chance of a home run. Failure is a great teacher, and if we view it from that positive perspective, we benefit from it. Failure should make us more curious, humbler, more empathetic, and more resilient—the Big 4 get bigger!

Recovering quickly from what you perceive as a failure, and perhaps what everyone around you perceives as a failure, requires that you've integrated every other major lesson in this book to some degree. To recover quickly, you need to continue to recognize opportunity, lead with heart, be prepared to move on, have a firm grasp of what you need to communicate, recognize both the wisdom and folly of certain opposition, and have people around you whose trust and loyalty you have earned.

One of the simple concepts in this chapter that can help you recover and get back on track with your leadership is considering how well you exercise what author Peter Block calls *stewardship*, that is "the willingness to be accountable for the well-being of the larger organization by operating in service, rather than in control of those around us."[1] That others-focused approach to leadership invites colleagues, board members, and constituents to take action to accelerate your recovery process. As Facebook executive and *Lean In* author Sheryl Sandberg has said, "We need to build resilience together." The irony is that some of those very people around you that you have counted on may be the cause of your temporary derailment. Hopefully the guidance in this chapter will help you untangle what may be a complex challenge involving the people around you.

Some of the hardest work you will ever tackle will be rebounding from a setback. It's easy to keep looking forward and moving ahead with strength and energy when you are riding high. It's easy to stay focused on what's next because the events that preceded it carry positive feelings. When things aren't going well—for you, for your team, and/or for your organization—your job as a responsive leader can get incredibly difficult. The decisions you face might seem harder to make, or even harder to identify, because your emotions have you in a head lock.

OPTIONS FOR THE REBOUNDING PROCESS

Because leaders have personality differences, ways of operating, and different sets of circumstances, no one formula will help you rebound. However, some or all of these options may help you accelerate your recovery from a little stumble or even a terrible failure of judgment.

One bit of guidance that applies no matter what your personal style pertains to pacing. Do not make hasty decisions. Sometimes a course of action will come quickly, but there is a big difference between decisiveness and hastiness. Many highly regarded people, including former US President Dwight D. Eisenhower, have been associated with the *24-hour rule.* The concept is to wait a day before making a major decision or to wait a day before responding to a professional associate who has been able to arouse your intense emotions. Unless the decision you must make is literally a life-or-death choice of action—in that case, you probably work in the emergency department of a hospital—take a deep breath. Do not assume your first response to an issue or challenge is the best.

Using the Five Stages

As mentioned in Chapter 5, psychiatrist Elisabeth Kübler-Ross is known for her five stages of dying: denial, anger, bargaining, depression, and acceptance. A leader who is familiar with these can use them as warning signs because the same experiences describe a career, or an entire organization, in a death spiral.

Mark had been the vice president of a large, prestigious art museum for ten years. He was nearing retirement age but would not be there for another five years. Mark's track record in luring large gifts was well-known in the community of nonprofit arts organizations. Unfortunately, so was his appetite for female coworkers and his penchant for losing control after drinking alcohol. Mark's boss and the board of trustees swept aside the first three sexual harassment complaints against him. In the final year of his employment, however, another two women accused him of inappropriate behavior. He was abruptly terminated.

Two months after he was fired, Mark called in a favor and got another senior position down the street from the museum. His new boss, the president of the organization, soon realized that Mark was returning to his old haunts—the bars and restaurants he frequented when he had been at the museum. In a tangible way, Mark was clinging to the environments and experiences he associated with his museum position—one of many manifestations of his denial. In addition, it was common for him to drink himself into a state of self-pity and depression. He also went out of his way to criticize the board and executives at the museum, holding them up as examples of failed decision-makers to the people in his new organization. His anger was palpable.

In terms of the Kübler-Ross stages, Mark bounced around but never made it to acceptance. Even after the president at his new company threw ice water on Mark's career when he fired him, Mark still wouldn't admit that his professional life had collapsed, and he continued to try to sell himself.

Now let's turn the Kubler-Ross model around and give *acceptance* a happy-ending meaning. Consider how a situation headed toward termination could have a different outcome if the leader facing challenges and problems recognizes some of the stages.

Unlike people facing physical death, it is sometimes possible to see the cycle beginning and initiate a miraculous recovery, or at least a respectable rebound. For example, say you recognize that you are in denial about problems and angry that you lack support for a project you value. You realize, "Whoa! I have to turn this around before the situation really gets out of hand." In contrast, you may do what some terminally ill patients do a for a long time: sustain a state of denial when acceptance of the inevitable would lead to a much easier transition.

I would recommend you keep a list of the Kübler-Ross stages handy as part of your "keep your bags packed" strategy. Periodically, go over them and ask yourself if you are denying the existence of problems, bargaining to try to make a bad situation better, or lashing out at anyone over getting in your way or hurting your feelings. Ask yourself if you feel discouraged—so discouraged that you might be described sometimes as depressed.

If so, it's decision time. And if you want to recover quickly—which could either lead to turning around the situation or departing in a timely manner—then replace the depression stage with a sense of mission. Instead of stages of death and dying, therefore, you can rely on stages of transition and decision:

Denial: Denial is a normal experience, especially for someone who has had a great deal of success and now faces challenges or even threats. "This can't be happening" is a logical, although unhelpful, response.

Anger: In the face of what you perceive as unreasonable opposition, anger is another normal, human response. No doubt your experience as a leader has involved you in many trying situations; however, if you can make sense of them, then you can move forward. When an attack seems outrageous and groundless, though, a burst of anger might be irrepressible.

Bargaining: The impulse to save your skin through "what if I did this?" and "how would you feel about that?" negotiation tactics is bargaining. Guilt—"If only

I'd done this or that, then none of this would have happened."—often propels this exercise because of a looming internal issue. An essential element in recovering quickly is forgiving yourself. Your may have made a misstep; all human beings do. Forgive yourself and move past it rather than revisit the mistake.

Mission Focus: It's time to take attention away from yourself and put it back on the organization. Whereas the Kübler-Ross stages include depression—a self-focused experience that is 100 percent legitimate if you face issues of death and dying—your challenge as a leader is to focus on others. Put your mind to work on the shared vision for the organization, the purpose for its existence, and what's best for its health.

Acceptance: Commit to a course of action. If the conclusion you reach during your mission-focused reflection is that you should stay, then pull your troops together and meet the challenge. If the conclusion you reach is that the organization would be better off without you, then walk out the door. Straddling the two options to see what might shake out does not mean you have accepted your reality. Acceptance is a positive, decisive move.

Establishing Mind Dominance

In the face of a threat, it is vital to stay in your human brain as much as possible. Adrenaline and cortisol kick in when you are in a state of fight or flight (the reptilian brain), which is only useful if you need to run or punch. The same autonomic nervous system responses can kick in even if you are not physically threatened. A person who thinks she is about to be fired from a job she wants to cling to could easily go into a state of fight or flight—but running away or punching the perceived perpetrator are not options for a working professional.

When the organization itself is charged with negative emotions such as fear or anger, your job as a leader is to get the organization out of that emotional state and focused on a planned, intentional, healthy strategy. You probably won't succeed if you are not there yourself.

Let's revisit the continuum I introduced in Chapter 5. In that context, it captured the range of possibilities related to the opposition, from purely emotional to thoughtful and logical. The same could be said about the opposition you pose to yourself. If you are dominated by emotion—or worse, by your most basic survival instinct associated with your reptilian brain—then you have a diminished capacity to solve problems with your thinking.

Emotion ◄──────────────────► Intellect

Intellect is about strategy. Get out of the anger and hurt, whatever is driving you emotionally, and move into strategy. Move into an action-oriented frame of mind.

One approach to problem-solving that has the potential to allow you to make this move is what author Deborah Schroeder-Saulnier calls *paradox thinking*. It is a proven path to help people think strategically and creatively, allowing them to back away from an emotionally driven response that comes out of taking sides on an issue. This process gets people to consider alternatives as though they are companion ideas rather than in opposition to each other. Schroeder-Saulnier explains: "Paradox thinking is 'and' thinking. It is thinking that identifies pairs of opposites and determines how they are interdependent relative to a key goal."[2]

We accept this as normal and natural in terms of everyday life. Inhale *and* exhale. Sleep *and* wake. Human beings don't do either one or the other of these things in order to live; we do both. Similarly, people in an organization can look at their organic needs and identify what opposites might actually be paired for the health of the company.

For example, let's say your organization has two, ostensibly conflicting goals: cut costs and invest in new programs. Your initial reaction might be, "That's impossible." Therein lies the magic of engaging in paradox thinking. By committing to a process wherein your team agrees to explore how to do both, you get everyone focused on a strategic exercise with a clear goal that puts both options in the arena of possibility.

Paradox thinking enables balanced management of conflicting objectives. *A company wants to be known for innovation at the same time customers embrace it for its stability, to thrill shareholders with strong short-term revenue results and, concurrently, to take action to ensure long-term health. From those examples alone, it should be easy to see how failure to manage a critical pair of opposites results in the company stumbling and, perhaps, falling.*[3]

You can't always have an *and*, but you need to know when it's a possibility. If it's even a remote possibility, explore it with the teams who are on opposite sides of the issue.

At Wheelock, an example of an *and* is the student center building project. In general, faculty felt that any investment should be made in them and the academic program, not student services. I would get pushback on something relatively inexpensive, such as hiring a new student counselor, if it meant not hiring a new faculty member. Can you imagine, then, the resistance I got with the notion of building a student center that would cost tens of millions of dollars? Even when I argued that without robust student services and other ways to attract new customers we'd have to cut the faculty rather than increase it, many told me I was wrong. Their thought was, "Nonsense. People will automatically come to the college if we have a strong faculty." Sure, like people come to a good restaurant in a run-down building on a remote road.

Without a process in place to bring the two sides together to consider options, emotions will run high and cooperation will run low. There will be no point of common focus to bring out the best of everyone's logic and creativity.

Over the years, Schroeder-Saulnier has refined the process she has used to help businesses effect remarkable turnarounds and dramatic gains in revenue and reputation. In brief, the two key opposites would be at the center of a graphic and be depicted something like this:

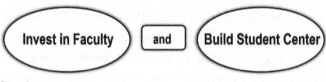

Paradox

The exercise would then involve the groups filling in the rest of the graphic with

- The likely benefits of investing in faculty and the benefits of building a student center

- The possible negative impacts of investing in faculty and those of building a student center

- What actions would be necessary to reap the benefits of each

- What metrics would apply in determining the success or failure of each course of action[4]

Let's say everyone is looking at the result of the two groups' input and sees that the only substantial downside to building the center is diverting money from other line items in the budget. A logical action step would be exactly what we did at Wheelock: set out to find money that wasn't in the budget—and would not ever be in Wheelock's hands if we did *not* build the center. That resulted in the $1 million donation for the planning we needed to ascertain our ability to design and build the center—the first measurement of success. The initial donation planted the seed that grew to $9 million to hire the design team and do the rest of the preparatory work. And that grew to $36 million to execute the plans.

One metric related to both the building and to faculty development was determining to what extent investment in both would stimulate interest in attending Wheelock. With "increased enrollment" being one of the college's three top goals during my tenure, this was a metric with long-term value in determining both *and* situations as well as *either/or* situations. A process such as that designed by Schroeder-Saulnier infuses decision-making with a scientific method that engages parties with conflicting ideas to think together—not just to work together.

With the expenditures side of the budget untouched by building activities, we could, indeed, achieve our *and*. Everyone on campus had reasons to get behind the project once the benefits of success were illuminated.

Putting Emotion in Its Place

Sometimes emotion is precisely what you need. Your strategy *is* an emotional response. If the opposition or threat to you involves your team or someone on your team, for example, your outrage or anger may serve you and the organization well.

During some personally difficult times at Wheelock, an event that triggered powerful, positive emotions helped me substantially. The emotion of the moment gave me strength, helped me restore a sense of purpose, and, yes, made me *think* more clearly about options. Here is what happened.

I was walking across Wheelock's campus toward my office one day. I was lost in thought and distracted by my own personal problems. I heard a voice say, "President Jackie!" I turned, and found a young African-American student approaching me. I didn't remember her. She gave me a hug and whispered in my ear, "I'm praying for you," and then she turned and walked away. I was stunned. That simple message changed my perception of my purpose for being at Wheelock. It reminded me of one of the most important roles that I was there to play. My role was to be a messenger that women of color could be the president of a college. That they could be anything they put their minds to.

That simple act turned me around and gave me the courage to continue on and to do the work boldly and with integrity.

Another emotionally charged moment gave me a message I still carry with me to this day: We are the bridge. We, leaders, are the bridge between the hopes, dreams, and aspirations of those who came before us and those who will come after us. You don't have to feel as though you are part of a persecuted minority, or any other kind of outsider, to appreciate the value of moving forward in your leadership as a bridge.

Every one of us who takes responsibility for our actions in some way—whether through leadership of an organization or by parenting the next generation—is a bridge.

In the middle of my darkest days at Wheelock, I received an award from The Harvard Club. I didn't want to accept the award, but I showed up on the designated evening. Shortly after arriving, I ran into a colleague. She said, "I came to see you receive your award." I started to say that I'd received too many awards already, and that there were so many deserving women who should be recognized. In other words, my emotional junk surfaced in technicolor.

She stopped me midsentence, pointed to the portraits of all white men hanging on the walls, and said, "Jackie, this is not about you. This is about our grandmothers, aunts, and all the unnamed women who cleaned their houses, washed their clothes, and cared for their children. This is about them. So you hold your head up high and gladly receive every recognition you are given."

She reminded me what this is all about. She changed my attitude about receiving recognition and I am so grateful for that wisdom.

We are the bridge. Each one of us links arms with those who came before us. We have a responsibility to build a strong and enduring bridge so that those who come after us can lead boldly and be the keepers of *our* dreams and aspirations.

8

Making Transitions

The pace of change and innovation, and the pressure to succeed financially, whether you are in a for-profit or not-for-profile environment, will force you to become a master of transitions. As leaders, we are always dealing with transition, whether we are creating a new plan, moving a project to the next stage, or restructuring a department. But as the world speeds up, so does the intensity of the transitions. Your integrity as a leader is the primary source of your backbone and judgment to be a master of transitions.

Integrity means honor, principle, honesty. If you adhere to very simple guidelines, then whether you are leading an organization through transitions or leading yourself through transitions, you will sail through with power and direction.

At the beginning of this book, I introduced the Big 4. As we enter a chapter that looks at the interplay of the 7 Secrets in going through transitions in your organization, I ask that you consider the Big 4 again. After exploring the 7 Secrets, do you find yourself understanding a little bit more how each of the Big 4 supports responsive leadership?

Curiosity: A desire to continuously learn, discover, and grow intellectually

Humility: A sincere regard for the reality that we cannot go it alone

Empathy: The ability to feel and appreciate other human beings

Resilience: The capacity to recover, to keep going forward in the face of adversity

This chapter is not a single lesson it itself, but rather a collection of lessons related to internal and external struggle. Let's first address the most defined transition, that is, moving out of your current position. How well you handle that affects your future prospects, of course, but it also affects the people around you and your own state of mind. What you absorb from the experience of leaving a job will help you avoid future catastrophes and use every work situation as an opportunity to build a stronger network.

The rest of this chapter is devoted to handling the most challenging transitions that occur while you are with an organization. In general, you can view these transitions as signs that your job is evolving—that's a very good thing unless you like a low-risk environment and can accept stagnation. As a leader, that probably sounds like career death to you, as it did to me.

WALKING OUT THE DOOR

My mother worked for General Motors for thirty-nine years. Today, that kind of relationship with a company is nearly unheard of. For the most part, people change jobs every few years, and that no longer applies just to entry level positions. In 2018, according to the US Bureau of Labor Statistics, the median number of years that salaried workers had been with their current employer was just 4.6 years. The average tenure of a college president is about 8 years, according to the American Council on Education. And while the CEO tenure appears to be getting slightly longer since the early 2000s, it's just 8.1 years as of this writing and bears a tight correspondence to increases in CEO salaries[1]—meaning that many CEOs are probably trying to stay in their jobs because they don't want to suffer a blow to their lifestyle.

What does transition mean to you if you're thirty years old? It means that you will probably have about a dozen more jobs before you retire. That kind of career path was unheard of by most people in my generation. In the thirty-five years before I launched my consulting practice, I held three jobs, with thirty-two of those years being in the president's chair. One of my friends, a fellow senior executive whose experiences were referenced anonymously in earlier chapters, has been in only five positions in forty years.

In short, the tenure of leadership is changing; apparently only those at the top who have large salaries and golden parachutes are seeing a slight extension in the lifespan of their C-suite experience.

The question you face is this: How will you apply the Big 4 in your transition to another position of responsive leadership? If you do it well, your move holds the promise of satisfaction for you and an infusion of quality leadership for the organization, regardless of how long that leadership lasts. But if you're out of balance—for example, far more curious than humble—you run the risk of diminishing job satisfaction and scrambling to move again, hoping to do it right the next time.

Learning from Longevity

Let's look at couple of departures made by long-time leaders to begin to explore not only when to transition out of a position, but also how to do it.

> *After growing up in public housing projects on Manhattan's Lower East Side, [Ursula] Burns began her career as an intern at Xerox in 1980. She was named chief executive 29 years later, becoming the first black woman to run an S&P 500 company. Under her watch, revenue shot up 50% from 2009 to 2011, reaching $23 billion. But it slid to $18 billion by the end of 2015. The following year, Xerox split its business into two companies and named two new CEOs, Jeff Jacobson and Ashok Vemuri. In an interview this summer, Burns said of her resignation, "I'm not sure why people are so shocked that someone who had been doing something for eight or 10 years would want to move on."[2]*

Burns had moved into senior roles at Xerox nearly fifteen years before she even became CEO in 2009. She was accustomed to the demands of senior leadership and the pressures, so when she was appointed CEO, she knew she deserved it. The fact that she was making history twice—by being the first African-American woman to run a company of this stature and by being the first woman to succeed a female CEO—did not seem to faze her. She was where she belonged and, as she mentioned in an interview with the *Financial Times* after her departure, she said it was really the media that made a big deal out of her gender, race, and the fact that she grew up poor.[3]

Like a good responsive leader, she didn't accept being singled out as the only one of "her kind" who could manage to become CEO of a major company. She turned the attention on the many other women and men of color who came from the projects who were just as qualified as she was and ready to step on to the global corporate stage:

> *I happened to be the one found at the time. The one that society as a whole allowed to play the game. There are a lot more people ready to play the game.*
>
> *There was a lot of discussion about how spectacular and amazing I was, and I decided—just recently—that the reason why those words were used is because it made it easier for you guys to accept me in. If I were an ordinary person, then you would have to start thinking about why I was the only person sitting there.*[4]

To the advice on seizing opportunities in Chapter 1, therefore, I would add what Burns implied in that statement. That is, if you are ready to play the game, let people know. Keep your head high and let everyone know you are ready. As a corollary, if you are seen as an outsider by some people once you've seized the opportunity, don't see *yourself* as an outsider. If you belong at the helm, then step up and start navigating the ship.

Burns could not escape the reality that her departure would leave a cultural void—that it represented more than an experienced, accomplished CEO resigning when the company found itself at a crossroads. When she left, not one black woman remained as CEO of any of the top-grossing US companies. Xerox took heat from some influential voices; the symbolism of her leaving was too great for them to bear. But Burns turned the discussion around, and by doing so, continued to be far more than a symbol.

When she left, Burns praised Xerox for leading the way: "We should be saying 'hooray' to the people of Xerox. We should be giving them a medal."[5]

Burns took her leadership to the boards of multiple, major companies, including Uber. More importantly, she is using her distinction of being the first African-American woman to run an S&P 500 company to improve US education in science, technology, engineering, and math (STEM).

Among the lessons she has about significant transitions, and ultimately walking out the door, are some of those you have seen in previous chapters:

- *Be a little more guarded about your words.* That's another way of saying that there are times when emotion and/or first thoughts aroused by a situation should not be expressed when they occur. In Burns' case, she was enjoying a morning walk around Central Park when her head of investor relations called her to alert her that Carl Icahn, known as a notorious corporate raider, was figuratively (and soon to be literally) at Xerox's front door. Over the next few days, this highly experienced CEO who had weathered transitions before and made tough decisions for years, sought the advice of her board and other people she trusted: "I had to be trained on how to be a little less Ursula Burns, and how to be a little more guarded."[6]

- *Don't take it personally.* Icahn's moves to take a relatively big chunk of Xerox stock threatened the very existence of the company that Burns had been with for decades. He intended to use his position to dismantle the company.

I had some great advice. It turns out, without this advice, everything would have turned out very differently. Simple advice someone told me: Don't take this personally.

. . . From his perspective, he's not taking it personally at all. It could have been me or Joe Schmoe sitting in my chair. He had a mission he was on and he was going to execute that to the best of his ability. [7]

- *Collaborate to whatever extent possible.* Despite the shark-like nature of Icahn's approach, Burns realized that no good would be served, for her or for her organization, if she either retreated or waged a futile battle. The best strategy was to lay out what she felt was a healthy plan for the company, listen to Icahn, and then see what they could identify as points of convergence. In my vocabulary, this is a great example of curiosity, humility, empathy, and resilience at work all at the same time. Without all of them in play, the drive would be to wash her hands of the mess and retire—as she had already planned to do anyway. Instead, she chose to listen, share ideas, respect her adversary, remain openminded, and through it all, keep a sturdy backbone. She said, "It was definitely tough, but it was one of the most intense learning experiences that I ever had." [8]

- *Take credit for the wins.* Your hard work and diligence may lay the foundation for someone else's success. Humility is not the same thing as modesty, so take credit. Humility will drive you to credit your team, but modesty will drive you to diminish the importance of your leadership in driving successes for your organization. At Xerox, Carl Icahn cashed in on some of the groundwork that Burns had already laid for splitting the company into parts—a service company and a hardware company. Burns was not shy about noting that this was a good idea that was not an Icahn original.

Burns' experience toward the end was bittersweet. She'd had a great, long run, but ultimately Ichan's shark attack made the onset of retirement a different experience from the usual evening of tributes and filet mignon. Fortunately, she is still with us as an educational leader, sharing the lessons of her corporate life with emerging leaders.

Another CEO whose tenure offers some enduring lessons for responsive leaders is Harlan Kent, the former CEO of Yankee Candle, who had been with the company for thirteen years when a takeover ousted him. In her book, *The Power of Paradox*, Deborah Schroeder-Saulnier profiled Kent because his curiosity made him ask himself how he could possibly hold down expenses while investing in growth—a seemingly impossible objective to achieve. He clearly had deep concern for holding his staff together as well as putting their talents and skills to good use to accomplish this goal. The result was a company that did what some experts thought was not possible. While many companies were driven to lay off staff due to the recession of 2008 and its resulting shock waves, Yankee Candle opened more than thirty stores a year and created many new jobs.[9]

How did he do it?

Focusing too much on cost containment has the potential to drive down entrepreneurial spirit—the lifeblood of consumer goods business like this—because it would be seen as embodying too much risk. Balancing his efforts to drive down expenses is his continuing support of a culture that has encouraged breaking out in new directions.

Kent himself took a risk to prove that he was open to new ideas to solve problems and find new creative paths. For the television show Undercover Boss, *he disguised himself as an entry-level employee in four roles: sales associate, packer, store manager, and second assistant manager. He made discoveries about when and how not to cut costs, what kind of leadership talent resided in someone who packed boxes of candles for the company, and much more. Such executive exposure to people who make the company hum on a daily basis is very likely to make it clearer how doing this and that—in this case, cost containment and growth—can be an achievable paradox that can engage employees at all levels.[10]*

Although she didn't use my Big-4 words, Schroeder-Saulnier is describing a curious, humble, empathetic, and resilient leader. During his tenure, Kent more than doubled Yankee Candle's revenues to $840 million and increased the company's market capitalization to $1.7 billion. I use this as one example of the Big 4 being part of a financially sound strategy for a leader.

Learning from Leaders Who Overlooked the Big 4

Many characteristics can undermine effective leadership, but two of the most pernicious are also two of the most common: ego and arrogance. Right here and now, I'm going to assert that systematic leaders are more likely to suffer from these attributes than responsive leaders are.

The very nature of systematic leadership involves imposing ideas and processes rather than inviting contributions to improve ideas and processes. At the same time, it is possible for a responsive leader to fall short—pushing more than one of the Big 4 aside for while—and suffer the consequences. I also provide an example of that in this section.

Both ego and arrogance played a role in the ultimate collapse of Toys "R" Us. The insider information on this comes from Christopher Byrne (*Funny Business* and *Toy Time!*), aka The Toy Guy. Byrne has spent his career focusing on the toy industry, primarily on the products of toy companies that have brought generations of people great joy. Byrne shared his insights on leadership with me for this book, which I found antithetical to the kind of leadership we might expect from an industry theoretically focused on making children happy. As part of that narrative, Byrne explained how low levels of curiosity and humility—empathy never appeared to be there—undermined the senior leaders' ability to be resilient. One leader after another was affected by a nebula that distorted his ability to perceive good advice, employ the talents of people around him, and create a successful business model.

> In the case of Toys "R" Us, ego landed the company with a gargantuan store in Times Square, and a sprawling office campus in Wayne, New Jersey, both in 2001. At the time, the retailer was reeling from losing out to Walmart as the largest toy store in the United States for the past two years, and it seemed as though both moves were statements being made by then-CEO John Eyler.
>
> Flashy they were, with a price tag in the tens of millions of dollars, but according to people who were there at the time,

the chain's founder Charles Lazarus strongly objected to these moves. They flew directly in the face of the company's core value of low-cost operations. Moreover, while the Times Square store was being developed, the focus of the entire company was diverted to opening one store, which changed the focus of the business—and not in a good way. The pursuit of the big, shiny thing, what we like to call "Magpie Management," is unfortunately all too common among ego-driven managers. It may look good to a board or make a cool news story, but all too often it dilutes, distracts, and disrupts the clear, effective running of a business.

Arrogance often arises when a putative leader insists that his or her vision is correct, without respect to what the market was indicating. In the case of Toys "R" Us, they were late to the party in online sales because CEO Robert Nakasone didn't believe in their potential. In 1997, total online sales would have been less than just one store in the chain, so Nakasone dismissed it. However, when eToys.com came along, and in the first day of its IPO in 1999 was, with approximately $30 million in sales for 1998, worth more, on paper, than Toys "R" Us with sales in the billions, it was a wake-up call. Well, it was more like the teenage game of fire drill, where kids are running around like lunatics piling into and out of a car at a red light.

The desperation led Toys "R" Us to make many disastrous choices to try to solve an out-of-control problem and led to Nakasone's resignation. In addition to the lack of vision, logistical missteps, and poorly executed deals, there was one other factor that was arrogance in action. Toys "R" Us had always been run by the merchants, people who knew toys and kids. It's more an art than a science, but under Nakasone, it began being run by MBAs. Experience, insight, and yes, gut gave way to data, models, and spreadsheets. The toy industry just doesn't work that way. After all, a company's business rises or falls at the whims of a child, and those are notoriously difficult to model.

The upshot of both events was that Toys "R" Us was in a weakened position, so it was ripe for the picking in 2005 when Bain Capital, Vornado Realty Trust, and Kohlberg Kravis Roberts orchestrated a leverage buyout. The problem was that the new company was so saddled with debt that it could never implement the improvements it needed to survive in a changing marketplace. The imagined IPO when everyone would cash out would never happened, and the company crashed into bankruptcy in 2018.[11]

As a responsive leader, you might read this narrative of the demise of Toys "R" Us and be horrified at self-serving actions that caused the loss of 31,000 jobs—31,000 people (who were making far less than executive wages anyway) abruptly cut off from employment. To make matters worse for those people, "Mass layoffs are usually softened with a severance package, but Toys 'R' Us employees won't get any because of bankruptcy laws."[12]

Unfortunately, I could provide you with dozens of examples just like this of leaders who drove their companies, both for-profit and not-for-profit, to destruction because they imposed their "solutions" instead of respecting the tenets of powerful, enduring leadership—the Big 4.

And then there was Wheelock. We had rousing successes for nearly a decade, and then over time, certain shifts in the composition of the board and staff signaled the beginning of an erosion of my leadership. The process calls to mind a story a friend told me about some property near her home just south of San Francisco. A young manager working in Silicon Valley bought some land, hoping to develop it when she had the money to build a home. Five years later, when she was prepared to begin building, she was told that water had been trickling through the property. Over time, a tiny creek had formed; as a result, a swath of her property was going to be declared a wetland, so she would be unable to build.

I know that sounds like a joke, but it's no more a joke than waking up one day to realize that the landscape of your career has changed so much that you can no longer plan or function the way you used to.

For the first twenty-five years of my career as a senior executive, while holding the titles of president and CEO, I never had to worry about being an outsider—in any way. My experience seemed to affirm my belief that hard work and outstanding results will overcome the need to be in "the club." If you're a driven person like me, and you share that belief, be careful: you may miss something. You may miss signals that you have lost ground and might even be on the way down or the way out. I missed those signals partly because I was still riding high in my tenth year at Wheelock, having received a sterling performance review that involved board interviews with thirty-five people. I let my curiosity ebb, not in terms of doing my job, but in terms of leading *myself*—my first job.

Even if you haven't felt like an outsider because your achievements have landed you in a sweet spot for promotion, election, honors, and prestigious appointments, others may see you as an outsider because they are focused on the differences between them and you. In other words, while you are going merrily along, doing the same outstanding job you've consistently done, you aren't aware that a few new people populating your world are infecting others—consciously or unconsciously—with a notion that your differences are important. Author Malcolm Gladwell (*Outliers*) addressed the gratuity that the insiders sometimes grant outsiders when they make an effort to be less different from the insiders: "Mainstream American society finds it easiest to be tolerant when the outsider chooses to minimize the differences that separate him from the majority. The country club opens its doors to Jews. The university welcomes African-Americans. Heterosexuals extend the privilege of marriage to the gay community."[13] In other words, in some environments, but you not only have to excel to be accepted, but you may also have to submerge a piece of your identity to get what you want.

By the time I realized that my Wheelock environment had transformed into an insider-outsider situation, it was too late. I was taking being shut out of executive committees personally. I was taking any challenge to my decisions personally. I didn't trust my resilience when it came to firing a senior staff member who actively sought to use her insider credentials to my detriment; I waited two years to do something that should have been done in the first two months she was on the job.

Looking back on the rocky days that preceded my departure, I can see that my ego got in the way. No, I wasn't as ego driven or callous as the Toys "R" Us CEOs as depicted in Byrne's narrative—whereas I lost focus of the Big 4, they completely ignored them. I continued to try to practice the 7 Secrets without the core characteristics that make them so effective.

The lesson is that you can never afford to let go of your core principles, the ones that keep you focused and help you seek out answers you may not want to know, and the courage to make hard choices.

STAYING IN AN EVOLVING ROLE

Very few leaders can sustain a fifty-year run the way Warren Buffett has at Berkshire Hathaway. Whether it's an organization a person founded, inherited, or took over at an early age, the ability to contribute substantially for decades is a rare phenomenon. My twenty-one years as president and CEO of Dimock surprised even me. I had intended to leave much sooner—on principle—but the fact is, my relationship with the mission of the organization, and the board and staff fulfilling that mission, continued to feel rock-solid.

When I came to Dimock, I thought that *job transition* meant moving to another job. A major donor of Dimock's who welcomed me to my presidency taught me otherwise. He was a successful real estate developer who quickly became a mentor for me and launched a productive relationship I had with the board through the shifts in board composition over the next twenty-one years.

Dan Rothenberg and I would have lunch about once a quarter. After I had been at Dimock for about ten years, I would occasionally say, "It's time to go." He was a wise man, a humble man full of curiosity and empathy, as well as a resilient businessman. Danny embraced and lived the Judaic concept of *Tikkun olam*, a desire to behave and act in a way that benefited his fellow man.

"Is it the same job?" he would ask me every time I brought this up at lunch. I would go back to my office and review what had happened, what we were going through, and what we looked forward to. The answer was invariably "no." In the twenty-one years I was at the helm at Dimock, I had about ten jobs. Roughly every two years, the challenges and objectives shifted substantially. As long as I could help the organization meet them—all the while making sure we were guided by the values of the organization—I realized I should stay at Dimock and do my job, as new and different as it became periodically.

I had the same title for twenty-one years, but not the same job.

When I first got to Dimock, we were rebuilding structures, upgrading facilities so we could better care for ill and injured people. The next major wave of need came with the AIDS crisis; the flow of sick and dying people from our community demanded an overhaul of services. Our answer to that need brought us in touch with organizations that had a national, and even global, outreach to address the growing public health concern that HIV posed. That helped us enter another developmental phase in which we focused on amplifying our reputation in the greater healthcare community; it enabled us to attract a new caliber of donors. Throughout these changes, we also had changes in board leadership and composition, again, with new people seeking out the opportunity to participate in Dimock's restoration. In turn, various successes enabled an impressive expansion of services, which meant a substantial increase in the number of staff members. The growth of our staff at Dimock is just one measure indicating how much change we went through—and how much my job was, in fact, many jobs—over the course of twenty-one years. We went from a staff of 60 when I began to 400 employees at the end of my tenure.

All of those major phases of growth and change required me to continuously learn and cultivate new skills. My initial job of infusing the Dimock community with reasons to believe we could return to stability and greatness turned into many jobs as we brought those reasons to life: new and restored buildings, new and more robust programs and services, new funding sources and innovative ways to reach a larger community of donors, new employees, and a restored reputation.

A memorable example of having one's job transform over and over again is the career of Sister Janet Eisner, who became president of Emmanuel College in 1979 and, as of this writing, still holds the post.

Sister Janet took the lead at Emmanuel the year the college turned sixty, and she has guided it through a series of clearly defined transitions over the decades. We might say that both the college and the president evolved in a Lamarckian way. Unlike Charles Darwin's perspective on evolution that involved change over generations, Jean-Baptiste Lamarck focused on evolutionary change that occurs within the lifespan of a single organism. The principle is called "change through use or disuse" and a classic example is a giraffe permanently lengthening its neck to reach the only edible leaves in its environment.

A quick look at the key events in the life of the college during Sister Janet's tenure in office suggests that, so far, she has had—to put it in Dan Rothenberg's terms—about sixteen different jobs in her forty years as president. Three of the transformative results of her evolution as president were tripling the enrollment on campus, bringing the campus physically into the twenty-first century, and turning the college into a coeducational institution. Among the many different jobs that led to those remarkable results were spearheading changes in organizational structure, initiating major building efforts, forging collaborative efforts with other institutions of higher learning and with the community, and forging an innovative partnership with a Fortune 100 company. Here are some of the highlights of her tenure at Emmanuel:

- Sister Janet stepped in when Emmanuel was still an all-women's college, and at a time women's issues were receiving an increasing amount of attention in the political arena. She took the college into the national spotlight during the 1984 Democratic presidential primaries when it hosted a debate on women's issues.

- Three years later, a new science center opened on campus—Sister Janet's first major building project.

- Over the next few years, the college invested steadily in infrastructure and accomplished something many colleges at the time could not boast of having: Emmanuel's campus became fully networked.

- In 1996, Sister Janet initiated the founding of the Colleges of the Fenway Consortium, a collaborative effort of five Boston-based colleges in the Fenway area, known primarily as the location of the ballpark that is home to the Boston Red Sox. Her concept was to offer students more opportunities for academic and social growth while still containing costs. Her vision has been a thriving effort that currently serves more than 12,000 undergraduates—16.2 percent of the total population of Boston undergraduate students.

- In 1998, a second major building project debuted when the College Chapel reopened after a complete renovation.

- Sister Janet ushered in the era of a coeducational experience with the dawn of the new millennium.

- In 2001, she negotiated a deal with Merck Research Laboratories, giving the pharmaceutical company a long-term lease on college land. She created both a revenue stream for the college and a groundbreaking partnership with a corporation that afforded Emmanuel students huge opportunities for learning and professional mentorship.

- Just a year later, the college established an institute to support urban education. The Carolyn A. Lynch Institute was analogous to our Mattahunt undertaking at Wheelock a few years later in that it brought students and faculty into an intimate relationship with its community so that they could have a positive impact on education.

- The next building project was completed in 2004—a student center with a dining hall, fitness facilities, and an NCAA-regulation gymnasium.

- Sister Janet's religious order, the Sisters of Notre Dame de Namur (SND), has a mission of social justice and education, "especially women and children, in the most abandoned places."[14] In 2007, Emmanuel established a center to bring more campus-wide action to fulfilling that mission.

- In 2009, Emmanuel restored the Roberto Clemente Field and turned it into their home turf for sports.

- Two other building projects followed closely on the heels of this sports facility upgrade, providing the college with a new science center and a renovated art department.

- Renovation of the college's historic Administration Building followed in 2013.

- In 2014, the college opened a new campus.

- In 2018, Sister Janet saw the culmination of an effort to form five academic schools: Humanities & Social Sciences, Science & Health, Business & Management, Education, and Nursing.

- Later that year, the college completed yet another building project when it opened a new eighteen-story apartment-style residence hall.

What's the key to her successful evolution—and the college's—that we can all learn from? In her Founders' Day address at Emmanuel College in 2011, Sister Janet reported that she had asked students and graduates from multiple classes what was key to their education at Emmanuel. She reported that the overwhelming response was "relationships." It comes down to people taking care of each other. That's not a soft, touchy-feely concept: it's the practical reality of practicing empathy, and empathy that is so widespread in a community reflects the principles of the leader.

When you research her career, it's easy to conclude that Sister Janet is a fiercely curious human being and that she is humble enough to have pulled teams toward her leadership to implement immense projects at the college. The fact that she has remained the president for four decades also suggests that she is resilient. As her board has changed, cultural norms have changed, and even the guidance from the Roman Catholic church has changed through the years, she has adapted and driven impressive growth in enrollment and reputation at the college.

Sister Janet's comment about the importance of relationships at Emmanuel suggests she might agree with

Lynne Azarchi that empathy is the gateway characteristic for the rest of the Big 4. Azarchi is executive director of the Kidsbridge Tolerance Center and author of an upcoming book on teaching empathy to children.

Her research has shown that empathy is dropping with the upcoming generations. An erosion of face-to-face people skills corresponds to our heavy reliance on electronic communication. This lack of empathy creates problems for employers, in part because some of these employees will ultimately prove their competence in job skills and earn promotions to positions of leadership. In a nutshell, that's not good for workplace health because "Little bullies become big bullies."[15] These are bosses who are driven by narcissism and a personal agenda. These are the leaders who impose systems on people without any concern for how disruptive or unproductive those systems might be.

Azarchi makes the following points to summarize how vital empathy is in the workplace, throughout every tier, from C-suite leadership to an intern who is just coming through the door straight out of college.

- Empathy is the foundation for workplace cooperation and productive collaboration. In most work environments, you need to work with other people—team members, customers, a boss.

- Empathy helps with inquiry and project-based learning. For this insight particularly, she credits Thom Markham (*Redefining Smart* and *Project Based Learning Handbook*) and notes how empathy in this context fuels curiosity and humility. In project-based learning, you are organized, working with teams, offering what you know, and openly inquiring about what you need to know. You are working with other people to get the information you need, and you wouldn't be asking if you weren't humble enough to realize you needed their help or knowledge.

- Empathy triggers creativity. Walking in the shoes of the customer is what gives rise to technology innovations such as those developed under Steve Jobs's leadership at Apple and products that make consumers enjoy their environment more such as those developed under Harlan Kent's leadership at Yankee Candle. The opposite of their empathy-drive approach is frightening for shareholders and employees—and it is well documented in the histories of many companies with failed launches. Gargantuan product mistakes resulted when customer needs and preferences were ignored. Let's start with Cheetos Lip Balm, move on to New Coke, round the corner with Harley Davidson perfume, and end up with Google Glass.

- Empathy increases employee retention. If we go back to Sister Janet's remark about the generations of Emmanuel graduates who target relationships as the vital force in their education, it's easy to see how the college is a model of how companies infused with empathy also thrive. People want to connect, to learn from each other, to assist each other, to perceive the aspirations and agendas of others as part of their own success. As a corollary, empathetic managers foster productivity.

- Empathetic leaders ask more questions—and therefore get more answers. Again, empathy serves as a foundational characteristic for the rest of the Big 4. Speaking on *The Late Show* with Stephen Colbert, when asked about the trait that leaders can't do without, acclaimed historian Doris Kearns Goodwin (*Leadership: In Turbulent Times*) responded that it was empathy. "Leaders need to understand other people, care about what others are feeling, and be able to communicate."[16] This is more than a situation such as Franklin Delano Roosevelt's literally understanding the challenges of having a physical handicap because he was afflicted with polio. It is a matter of putting action behind emotion to *want* to connect with people affected by your leadership, such as Lincoln did with slaves, and then truly listening. If Lincoln had not asked the hard questions, he would not have gotten the hard answers about emancipation. And without empathy, he would not have absorbed the answers.

As a leader, consider how much you would rely on all of the Big 4 to manage your own professional growth, as well as your organization's, during such dramatic changes. Every time, a substantial opportunity presented itself, you would not only need to respond with a strategy to succeed, but also with tactics.

- **Curiosity** will drive you to determine how the organizational structure needs to adapt. Your curiosity would demand that you do research— study other organizations that have exploited a similar opportunity, learn from past mistakes, ask for insights and critiques from your board members and other trusted counselors. Your curiosity will help you find ways to maintain the values of the organization while you are leading the transformation of its structure and operations.

- **Humility** will give you the capacity to modify your strategy based on new information and resources. It will compel you to acknowledge the talents and skills of people around you and how they will contribute to tactical success in carrying out your mission. Humility will strengthen you for any opposition you encounter; it will allow you to ask honestly for reasons behind that opposition rather than taking them personally, brushing them aside because they are in your way.

- **Empathy** will keep you tuned in to the impact that the dramatic changes are having on the people around you—staff, board, customers, clients, constituents, stakeholders. That awareness is vital to both the design and implementation of your strategy. It helps you refine tactics such as firing people with dignity and responding to the concerns and needs of people who are on the fringes of your peripheral vision. For example, at Dimock we faced the challenge of displacing the homeless people that were using one of our buildings as shelter if we proceeded with plans to locate a new program in that structure. Boston weather is not kind in the winter, and it doesn't necessarily offer warm and cozy nights even in the middle of summer. Those people counted on us, whether or not they were invited to sleep in that building, and I felt it was incumbent on us as a community institution to build a new element into our implementation plan: find a place for them to stay, at least for a while. (We weren't as concerned about the squirrels we also "asked" to vacate the building.)

- **Resilience** gives your strategy backbone. In leading any major change, you will encounter some kind of opposition, even if it's just from contrarian thinkers. As you lead the implementation process of your organization's transition, use your curiosity, humility, and empathy to their fullest value. They will fuel your resilience no matter what you encounter.

A primary, revenue-boosting outcome of using the Big 4 as a foundation for your leadership is seeking diversity in your organization. Homogeneity of ideas gave us the demise of Eastman Kodak and failed products that reflected the "good" ideas of countless celebrities. These are businesses such as actress Natalie Portman's well-intentioned vegan-friendly footwear. Let's applaud her for having good intentions, but not for having the curiosity, humility, and empathy to encircle herself with people who could help her succeed. As a result, resilience as a leader was unachievable; there was no bouncing back with that business model.

With the Big 4 in mind as you use the 7 Secrets outlined in this book, you will shape an organizational culture of inquisitiveness, collaboration, trust, and backbone. Even when you make a bad decision—and you will—you will be equipped to shoulder the responsibility rather than place blame. You will also pick yourself up and resume forward movement quickly because you will forgive your-self, just as you would forgive people who work for you and fail while they are doing the best they can.

You will lead by example and, by doing so, cultivate another generation of responsive leaders.

Conclusion:
The "I" in Leadership

There is no "I" in *team,* but there is an "I" in *leadership.* Early in this book, I told you that leading yourself is your first job. Unfortunately, sometimes great leaders fall short because they care so much about their projects and people that they start putting them first all the time. One of the things I briefly sacrificed at Wheelock because of my passion for getting a job done and keeping my team motivated was leading myself. That's a mistake. *Thriving* is a desired personal attribute as well as a goal for the institution. There is a connection between a leader's overall well-being and the well-being of the business.

The Big 4 can come to your rescue if you realize you are submerging your needs for the good of the organization or the success of the project. If anyone you trust makes a passing comment like, "When was the last time you had a vacation?" or "I haven't seen you go out for lunch in a while," then you might want to hear that as a kind reminder that you have removed the "I" from your leadership.

Some personal ways the Big 4 can bolster your mental, emotional, and physical vigor might be captured in these points:

- **Curiosity keeps you interesting to yourself as well as others.** Commit to being a continuous learner. You didn't get to your current position of leadership by leaving college and saying to yourself, "I know it all now." You won't hold on to your current position of leadership by saying that either.

   Periodically take inventory of what you listen to and read on a regular basis. Don't be embarrassed to admit that you enjoy a little pop-culture reading; it keeps you tuned in to cultural issues and priorities that open your mind to ideas that may be a little foreign to it. Indulge yourself by listening to a TED Talk while you're having a cup of coffee.

   You don't have to be taking online graduate school courses to keep your mind energized and your conversation interesting. Just do as much as you can to keep expanding your mental horizons—and giving your brain a change of pace from the problem-solving related to your job.

   Continuous learning is one of the key ingredients to becoming, and remaining, a person of substance—someone who realizes your words have meaning, does your best at all times, and is confident but not arrogant.

- **Humility lets other people make your life easier.** Hanging on to tasks because you do them better than anyone else will just make you an overworked, frustrating, uninspiring leader. You will be resented by people for robbing them of the opportunity to grow and improve, and ultimately, they will stop trying to kick in any effort to help you with "your" tasks. Another result of lacking humility could be that you can't handle the fact that someone else is doing your tasks better than you.

I know the founder of an organization who was a brilliant fundraiser. Her grant proposals had earned her educational institution millions of dollars. After a few years of going it alone, she finally decided to hire someone to help her raise money—someone who hit the ground running and immediately started getting corporate and foundation grants. The founder shut down. Instead of appreciating that she had a collaborator she could mentor, as well as learn from, she withdrew from fundraising and essentially stranded her competent new hire. Her lack of humility hurt her, and it hurt the organization. Fortunately, that's not the end of the story. With the help of one of her board members, she discovered how much strength can be found in humility. Among the benefits, she decided to take her first vacation in six years, confident that someone was capably writing grant proposals.

- **Empathy is a two-way street; it makes others feel good and it makes you feel good, too.** When someone else perceives that you understand him and the two of you are communicating on the same wave length, the pleasure centers of the brain light up for both of you. Both of you will de-stress and sense an increase in the level of trust between you.

- **Resilience requires self-love.** The balance and sense of well-being you need to be a resilient leader require you to care deeply about yourself. Although any gender can be afflicted by it, female leaders are particularly susceptible to what psychologist Harriet Braiker, a frequent guest of Oprah Winfrey's, calls the "disease to please." When you value everyone else's comfort over your own, you reduce your own ability to survive and thrive. When the mask drops down from the ceiling of the aircraft that's depressurized, you put it on the person next to you. He lives; you pass out.

  On a psychological level, part of self-love means not comparing yourself to other senior executives or others in your circle. It means saying, "no" to a spontaneous meeting that eats into your private time. A good rule for your psychological health is to find time every day for personal reflection; you need to be consistent about this. You can roll this time into a walk about the block or when you're listening to music—but do it daily.

  On an emotional level, loving yourself means forgiving yourself, not beating yourself up for mistakes. In an article called "Self-care Isn't Selfish—It's Essential for Our Resilience," this wonderful insight appears: "Letting go of what has happened and moving forward is key to our resilience. It takes energy to maintain a grudge or resentment. A wise person once said holding onto resentments is like allowing someone to live rent-free in your mind."[1]

On a physical level, it means nurturing your health. I'm a walker. It turns out that is a very healthy thing to be. In fact, an article in *Prevention* magazine talked about "10 Amazing Health Benefits of Walking 30 Minutes a Day, According to Doctors."[2] Here are three of those benefits:

- Your mood will improve.

- Your creative juices will start flowing.

- Your other goals will start to seem more reachable.

Walking, of course, is something you do in addition to other ways you promote your physical health. And if you're sick or worried about being sick, well then you aren't much good to the people around you, are you? So, if you're like me, you *must* (that's a strong imperative, chosen deliberately!) walk to clear your head. It is an activity that fuels the ability to lead.

Embrace the myriad benefits to you—and your organization—of putting a *capital* "I" in your leadership. As the US Army says in its long-time recruiting slogan, "Be all you can be." When you are, then you are the best leader you can be.

A

Exercises in Seeking Opportunities

EXERCISE

Envision what you think is your ideal position at this point in your life. Ask yourself, "Why me?" and then use the organizing principles to determine whether or not you're a match for it. If not, in which area do you think you fall short—people, places, things, or time?

Discussion

You have learned the senior leadership position in fundraising at a museum in San Francisco is open. You have a twelve-year track record in raising big money but very little experience interfacing with board members or leading a team. You currently live in Omaha, Nebraska.

Here is an approach to analyzing whether or not this is a good opportunity for you.

People

Pro: You are highly regarded at key funding organizations and have been successful before in connecting with people capable of making major gifts.

Con: You have very little sense of the politics of working with a board of trustees.

Places

Pro: You are willing to move to San Francisco.

Con: You currently live in a city with one of the lowest costs of living and would be moving to a city with one of the highest.

Things

Pro: Your skills in raising money are undeniable.

Con: Your experience in having a leadership role in raising money is limited.

Time

Pro: You have the more than a decade of the experience required to do a key part of the job and have proven in previous environments that you adapt quickly to new demands.

Con: You cannot point to years of leadership experience as a qualifying trait.

EXERCISE

Make a list of qualities, actions, or remarks by someone with whom you'd have to work closely that would set off alarms for you. What would push you over the edge—regardless of a fabulous salary and/or prestige—in deciding not to take a job.

Now flip that around. What qualities, actions, or remarks do you want to observe and hear? What would transform your opinion of a career move, taking it from desirable to spectacular—or from average to wonderful?

In considering these contrasting scenarios, try to think of how all four disclosure areas play a role in your analysis.

Discussion

Fortune magazine published a list called the Human Capital 30—companies that have an unusually low turnover rate due to the way they treat their employees. The list represents a wide range of industries: technology, finance, healthcare, energy, construction, hospitality, legal services, and more. Probably the most legendary of them is W. L. Gore & Associates, which makes Gore-Tex and Glide dental floss. Their reputation for being a fun and satisfying place to work has led to a voluntary turnover rate of an astonishing 3 percent. If you are aware that the company you are interviewing with has made this list, you might well choose it over a company like Amazon, where the median tenure is just one year. That said, you may choose to go to a company with high turnover for a great salary, the experience, and the connections you need to move to a better environment.

Interestingly, Deloitte's Global Human Capital Trends 2016 research targeted five ways that companies can build a great culture and have elements of people, places, things, and time threaded throughout. Clarity about goals, when you are expected to achieve them, who you will be working with, and what the rewards are of succeeding ranks high. A sense of place in the company also leads to satisfaction—that is, with your particular set of skills and talents, you might be energized by knowing that you can be mobile and agile within the organization.

EXERCISE

If you consider yourself skilled at turning a situation around, what problem would you most like to solve in your job as a leader and how might you go about it?

If your thrill comes more from escalating the success of an organization to cosmic proportions, what measures would you use to determine you had achieved that success?

Discussion

To stimulate your thinking about evaluating opportunities in relation to what success you're likely to achieve, let's look at the success profile of someone who is not a responsive leader: Donald J. Trump. His stated objective was to effect a turnaround in the operation of the United States government by serving as president. Since taking office in January 2017, his leadership would be considered a failure using any criteria involving the Big 4. However, using a largely quantitative set of criteria, his presidency would be evaluated differently.

For an article in *Forbes*, Sally Percy of The Institute of Leadership and Management analyzed US President Donald J. Trump's stature as a leader based on the Institute's Five Dimensions of Leadership: achievement, authenticity, collaboration, ownership, and vision. In her analysis, she was careful to define the criteria for each because she clearly was not a fan of Trump's. For the most part, she had a distinctly quantitative orientation, describing exactly what I called systematic leadership in the Introduction. With that in mind, here is how Trump fared:

- On the basis of his extraordinary fame, money, and power, Trump scores high in the area of achievement.

- If authenticity is defined as meaning what he says and saying what he means, then he scores high in this area, too.

- Whether or not he can collaborate depends to some extent on whether the focus is international or domestic. On the international stage, he scores low. Domestically, the score varies. He obviously doesn't give much weight to collaborating.

- Ownership is tricky because part of a leader's triumph is ensuring that others take ownership. Trump himself takes ownership, but he does little or nothing to support shared ownership.

- Vision? Heck, yes, he has vision, whether you like it or not: "Make American Great Again."

To summarize Percy's findings, President Trump did quite well in this evaluation, which she prefaced by saying that she wanted to be "as objective as possible."[1]

Using both the responsive leader and the systematic leader measures to consider success, tackle the preceding two exercise questions.

EXERCISE

Choose two major companies, one product and one service, and answer the question, "Where did it come from?" Ideally, choose companies that you know have been around at least a few decades and then research their history. Any surprises?

What was the role of certain people in shaping the company's purpose? Was that purpose tied to a location? To events at the time that created a need? To certain discoveries or inventions?

Discussion

You might start by looking at those lists of companies with high and low turnover rates. Focusing on companies that either hold on to employees or send them through a revolving door should give you a lot of insights into how you might view the "opportunity" to work within them if you want to be a responsive leader. To reiterate what I said in the Introduction, responsive leaders are very focused on the people—the humanity—within the opportunity.

B Communication Tools and Techniques

This appendix covers tools of structure and key communication techniques.

TOOLS OF STRUCTURE

Martin Murphy *(No More Pointless Meetings)* is an expert on turning meetings into productive communication sessions. His company, QuantumMeetings, has provided valuable workflow management tools to multi-billion-dollar companies as well as many not-for-profits and government entities. His opening advice—the most fundamental tool of structure—is to decide which of these types your meeting is:

- The *Issues Management Session* is designed to bring issues that must be addressed to the surface. In some cases, you can move to resolve the issue immediately by creating an Action Plan indicating who is responsible and what the due date is. In others, you move the issue to one of the next two sessions.

- An *Innovation Session* addresses issues that require new thinking or a new direction.

- The *Problem-Solving Session* tackles problems. Murphy draws a distinction between issues and problems and cautions against using the words interchangeably: "All problems are issues, but not all issues are problems."[1]

Use these distinctions as your basis for calling people together; then employ the tools of structure related to the session itself:

- Agenda

- Reports supporting the agenda

- An organizing procedure for meetings

- A "lectionary" for messaging

Agenda

Write it down. In meetings with my leadership team and board, we always had a written agenda, even if it contained just three items. This is counter to my natural style, and that's why it's so necessary for me. I enjoy applying my imagination to the future, brainstorming about possibilities and options. There is a time and place for that—the Martin Murphy Innovation Session—but that is not in a meeting in which it's vital to communicate a message to motivate people to take action. After a vote is taken that authorizes the action you want, however, you might want to adjourn and then move to an exciting, exploratory conversation about what's next.

You may be thinking, "Tell me something I don't know," so I will tell you a story that illuminates the way an agenda supports your leadership on a day-to-day basis.

I was consulting with a company in which a young CEO was not getting the respect of his office from a new director of operations. I asked him to describe his interactions with her and he said, "We huddle every morning, so she can tell me what's going on."

Here's the problem: she controlled those "huddles" by virtue of the fact that she chose what information to give him. She could establish what priorities were on the docket for the day by what she covered and what she emphasized.

I suggested he formalize his meetings with her. Instead of meeting casually every morning, they moved to a ninety-minute meeting once a week in which he established the agenda and they both had a copy of it in writing. He quickly regained his ground and engaged her in an even more productive way.

Reports

Whether it's you or someone on your team doing the reporting, ensure the four areas of disclosure are covered: people, places, things, and time. Check yourself and others on the following:

- Answering all the "who" questions related to the issue. Who is accountable, responsible, in charge, on target with deliverables, . . . ?

- Answering all of the "where" questions. Where is the work being done, where will the service be performed, . . . ?

- Answering all the "what" questions. What problem are you solving, what are the components of the project, . . .?

- Answering all "when" questions with timelines, target dates for deliverables, and all of the other relevant time elements, including any important notes about the history of the effort.

A major shortcoming I've seen in reports is their lack of completeness because one or more of the areas of disclosure aren't covered. Use them to organize your thoughts, and to coach people in organizing theirs, and then create the report.

Organizing Procedure

I'm not a fan of parliamentary procedure, also known as Robert's Rules of Order. In my opinion, its primary value is in a setting with a highly contentious atmosphere— and if that's what you have, then as a leader, you should be turning your attention toward eliminating the cause rather than reining in the result.

Whatever procedure you create or adopt for your team, stick to it. One women's organization I know of has the simple, organizing principle of "old business, new business." The procedure that goes with it is consensus-building. I have seen lots of descriptions of how to do consensus-building in the context of a meeting, but I think the cleanest approach is in a book called *Rangers Lead the Way: The Army Rangers' Guide to Leading Your Organization*

Through Chaos, by former Army Ranger and leadership consultant Dean Hohl. Hohl recommends the following:

- Establish a ground rule at the start of the meeting that silence equals consent.

- Everyone must have the opportunity to speak.

- Those who choose to participate must feel as though they are accurately understood. To do this, whoever is leading the meeting has to commit to paraphrasing any contributions that aren't absolutely clear to the rest of the group—no exceptions and no assumptions!

- They must feel as if their ideas and contributions are seriously considered.[2]

After that, the group gives a pro or a con to the idea at hand.

Lectionary

As a responsive leader, you are always looking for ways to reinforce the vision and purpose you share with your team, board, constituents, and others. The concept of a *lectionary,* or linking certain messages with certain days or occasions, can help do that in a meeting.

This is something you can have fun with that also can add value. For example, you called an Innovation Meeting to brainstorm ideas for a fundraising event for your hospital. You kick off the meeting by announcing that, on this day in 1873, French chemist Louis Pasteur was awarded a patent for brewing beer and ale—even though he was mostly known for breakthrough discoveries in the causes and prevention of disease. You are on point with your theme in reminding the group why you are doing the fundraiser, and at the same time, you have set a tone of playful exploration.

KEY COMMUNICATION TECHNIQUES

You can get very sophisticated about communication techniques; whole books have been written about the topic. My simple advice here is this: use verbal and non-verbal techniques to keep people focused on the topic at hand and to invite their open communication with you.

The critical verbal technique is *mastering the point*. By that, I don't mean that you are an expert in the subject being discussed, but that

- You are clear on what is being discussed.

- You know enough about it to ask good questions.

- Whatever thoughts or opinions you have about the topic are organized in your mind. You can cover the four areas of disclosure—people, places, things, and time—in explaining your insights.

- You have a command of what your group understands.

- You know what stimulates discussion with your group.

A really important piece of *body language* you need to know is the difference between open and closed movements. Barriers help define personal space, but there are times when you want to avoid them. Responsive leadership means communicating that you are open to the ideas and opinions of other people, and a misuse of barriers gets in the way.

Barriers sometimes convey a sense of importance and power and they can make you can look unapproachable. They can also make you look weak and afraid—as if you're hiding behind something. When you use a desk, the angle of your body, a mobile phone, or anything else as a wedge between you and another person, you send a signal that you are closing yourself off on some level. While you are in a meeting of any size, be aware that invitational body language—that is, reducing or eliminating barriers—is an excellent, nonverbal way of communicating, "I'm listening."

C Organizing Information

I n this series of guidelines, I have built on the work of James O. Pyle, who wrote books about both questioning and responding to questions. What I develop in brief here is what he originally created for his interrogation students at the Survival, Evasion, Resistance, and Escape (SERE) school. The school is designed for US military personnel who have a high risk of capture by enemy troops—and there may be days during the tenure of your leadership that you feel besieged by enemy troops. Pyle's work morphed into something designed primarily for people in business in the book *Find Out Anything from Anyone, Anytime.*

The information found here is valuable in structuring reports of all kinds, but I mentioned it earlier in the book in relation to challenging personnel issues—the bullies, bigots, and others who give you and your ideas emotion-based opposition that is unhealthy and unproductive. For your own sanity, as well as for possible termination action later, you must have your thoughts about this opposition well documented.

I've already mentioned numerous times that the four areas of discovery/disclosure are people, places, things, and time. To go deeper into how you might subdivide those categories in the context of your responsive leadership and the challenges we face in our organizations, here are some guidelines.

PEOPLE

Using the Big 4 as a set of characteristics for understanding someone, how would you describe a person who seems to be opposing you needlessly or otherwise causing disruption in your team? Figure out where they might fit on a continuum involving each characteristic.

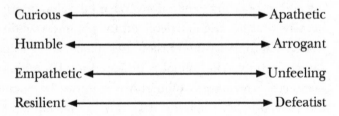

Curious ⟵⟶ Apathetic

Humble ⟵⟶ Arrogant

Empathetic ⟵⟶ Unfeeling

Resilient ⟵⟶ Defeatist

PLACES

In describing a place, include as many of these elements as are relevant:

- Directions

- Location

- Appearance

- Layout

- Function

THINGS

Things that are tangible are mechanical, electronic, structural, or expendable—or some combination of them, such as a car. The things you'll probably find yourself talking about most, however, are intangibles. They are processes like grant writing and concepts like revenue.

TIME

You might look at time as

- A single moment or date

- A chronology of events

- A period or era defined by certain characteristics or events

Consider how you could use this organizing principle of the four areas of discovery/disclosure in making a case for promoting someone. You want someone who scores well on the measures of curiosity, humility, empathy, and resilience.

- Where did you observe some of these characteristics at their strongest? The list of places might include an offsite meeting with a client, or an in-house training session on a new product line.

- What did the person do that impressed you so much? Maybe he explained the functionality of the company's new accounting software or made an inspiring pitch for funding a new program.

- When did the qualities seem most pronounced to you? Did you observe them getting stronger over time, or was there a turning point?

Using the four areas to organize information is a quick and efficient way to help yourself make the strongest case possible for whatever you are trying to achieve.

Notes

CHAPTER 1

1. Patricia Moore, "Patricia Moore—2012 RIT Innovation Hall of Fame," RIT Production Services, June 13, 2012, YouTube video, https://www.youtube.com/watch?v=cpNlBML2FFo.

2. Moore, " RIT Hall of Fame."

3. Moore, " RIT Hall of Fame."

4. Linda Dahlstrom and Jennifer Warnick, "Schultz to Employees: 'This Has Been the Dream of a Lifetime,'" Starbucks.com, June 5, 2018, https://stories.starbucks.com/stories/2018/schultz-to-employees-this-has-been-the-dream-of-a-lifetime/.

5. Steven R. Weisman, "Powell Calls His U.N. Speech a Lasting Blot on His Record," *New York Times*, September 9, 2005, https://www.nytimes.com/2005/09/09/politics/powell-calls-his-un-speech-a-lasting-blot-on-his-record.html.

6. Biography.com Editors, "Colin Powel," Biography.com, A&E Television Networks, April 17, 2019, https://www .biography.com/people/colin-powell-9445708.

7. Jason M. Breslow, "Colin Powell: U.N. Speech 'Was a Great Intelligence Failure," *Frontline*, PBS, May 17, 2016, https:// www.pbs.org/wgbh/frontline/article/colin-powell-u-n -speech-was-a-great-intelligence-failure/.

8. Jessica Thomas, "Roxbury," City of Boston, May 15, 2019, www.boston.gov/neighborhood/roxbury.

9. Alison Doyle, "How Often Do People Change Jobs?" The Balance Careers, January 29, 2019, https://www .thebalancecareers.com/how-often-do-people-change -jobs-2060467.

10. "Mission Statement," *Economist*, June 2, 2009, https:// www.economist.com/news/2009/06/02/mission-statement.

CHAPTER 2

1. Brené Brown, "Listening to Shame," TED 2012, March 2012, https://www.ted.com/talks/brene_brown_listening_to _shame.

2. Lawrence K. Altman, "Heterosexuals and AIDS: New Data Examined," *New York Times*, January 22, 1985, https:// www.nytimes.com/1985/01/22/science/heterosexuals -and-aids-new-data-examined.html.

3. John Gapper, "The Perils of the Chief Who Stays Too Long at the Top," *Financial Times*, April 16, 2014, https://www.ft.com/content/aee47536-c48f-11e3-8dd4 -00144feabdc0.

CHAPTER 3

1. Anonymous, "The Board Just Fired Me . . . and I'm the Founder!" *Blue Avocado*, May 28, 2011, https://blueavocado .org/board-of-directors/the-board-just-fired-me-and-i-m -the-founder/.

2. "Atlanta Native John O. Boone, Massachusetts' First Black Commissioner of Corrections Dies at Age 93," *Atlanta Daily World,* December 3, 2012, https://atlantadailyworld .com/2012/12/03/atlanta-native-john-o-boone-massachusetts -first-black-commissioner-of-corrections-dies-at-age-93/.

3. Jim McCormick and Maryann Karinch, *Business Lessons from the Edge* (New York: McGraw-Hill, 2009), 40.

4. McCormick and Karinch, *Business Lessons,* 40.

5. Norman Boucher, "The Simmons Legacy," *Brown Alumni Magazine,* May/June 2012, https://www.brownalumni magazine.com/articles/2012-05-24/the-simmons-legacy.

6. Boucher, "Simmons Legacy."

7. Andy Rowell, "What the Hell Did We Do to Deserve This?" *Oil Change International,* April 30, 2010, http://priceofoil .org/2010/04/30/%e2%80%9cwhat-the-hell-did-we-do -to-deserve-this%e2%80%9d/.

8. BBC News, "BP Boss Tony Hayward's Gaffes," BBC News Service, June 20, 2010, http://www.bbc.com/news /10360084.

9. Tim Webb, "BP Boss Admits Job on the Line Over Gulf Oil Spill," *Guardian,* May 14, 2010, https://www.theguardian .com/business/2010/may/13/bp-boss-admits-mistakes -gulf-oil-spill.

10. climatebrad, "BP CEO Tony Hayward: 'I'd Like My Life Back,'" YouTube video, May 31, 2010, https://www.youtube .com/watch?v=MTdKa9eWNFw.

11. Docmentation of this is found in numerous news articles and consolidated in the book *Deepwater Deception* (Washington, DC: WND Books, 2017) by Robert Kaluza, a survivor of the *Deepwater Horizon* blowout who was accused by the company and the US Department of Justice and exonerated of all wrong-doing related to it.

12. Dr. Marta Rosa, interview with author, December 5, 2018.

CHAPTER 4

1. William J. Clinton, "William J. Clinton Quotes," Brainy Quote.com, https://www.brainyquote.com/quotes/william _j_clinton_454934. Accessed December 9, 2018.

2. Jonathan Turetta, "Steve Jobs iPhone 2007 Presentation (HD)," YouTube video, May 13, 2013, youtube.com/watch ?v=vN4U5FqrOdQ.

3. Turetta, "Steve Jobs."

4. Google Developers, "Project Glass: Live Demo at Google I/O," YouTube video, June 27, 2012, https://www .youtube.com/watch?v=D7TB8b2t3QE.

5. Rev. Dr. Carolyn Wills, interview with author, September 23, 2018.

6. "Technology Evangelist UI/UX," Apple job posting, Glassdoor, August 28, 2018, https://www.glassdoor.com/ job-listing/technology-evangelist-ui-ux-apple-JV_ IC2940587_KO0,27_KE28,33.htm?jl=2888659029&ctt =1547247131851&srs=EI_JOBS. Accessed July 19, 2019.

7. Tristan Greene, "The First iPhone: What the Critics Said 10 Years Ago," The NextWeb (TNW), June 29, 2017, https://thenextweb.com/apple/2017/06/29/the-first-iphone-what-the-critics-said-10-years-ago/.

CHAPTER 5

1. Peter H. Lewis, "The Executive Computer; So Far, the Newton Experience Is Less Than Fulfilling," *New York Times,* September 26, 1993, https://www.nytimes.com/1993/09/26/business/the-executive-computer-so-far-the-newton-experience-is-less-than-fulfilling.html.

2. Natasha Geiling, "The Confusing and At-Times Counterproductive 1980s Response to the AIDS Epidemic," Smithsonian.com, December 4, 2014, https://www.smithsonianmag.com/history/the-confusing-and-at-times-counterproductive-1980s-response-to-the-aids-epidemic-180948611/.

3. Edward J. Koch, "Senator Helms's Callousness Toward AIDS Victims," *New York Times,* November 7, 1987.

4. Lymari Morales, "Obama's Birth Certificate Convinces Some, but Not All, Skeptics," *Gallup,* May 13, 2011, https://news.gallup.com/poll/147530/obama-birth-certificate-convinces-not-skeptics.aspx.

5. Julia Glum, "Some Republicans Still Think Obama Was Born in Kenya as Trump Resurrects Birther Conspiracy Theory," *Newsweek,* December 11, 2017, https://www.newsweek.com/trump-birther-obama-poll-republicans-kenya-744195.

6. Gerard Wynn quoting Al Gore in "U.S. Corn Ethanol 'Was Not a Good Policy,'" *Reuters,* November 22, 2010, https://

www.reuters.com/article/us-ethanol-gore/u-s-corn-ethanol
-was-not-a-good-policy-gore-idUSTRE6AL3CN20101122.

7. Earl E. Devaney, Inspector General, United States Department of the Interior, in a memorandum to Secretary Dirk Kempthorne, September 9, 2008, released to the public September 10, 2008, page 2.

8. John Ballard, interview with author, December 22, 2018.

9. Ballard, interview.

10. University of Cincinnati, "Understanding Bullying Behavior," https://behavioranalysis.uc.edu/understanding-bullying -behavior/, Accessed December 2018.

11. *Star Trek: Voyager*, Season 4, Episode 10, "Random Thoughts," directed by Alexander Singer, written by Kenneth Biller, created by Gene Roddenberry, Rick Berman, Michael Piller, and Jeri Taylor, featuring Kate Mulgrew, Robert Beltran, and Roxann Dawson, aired November 19, 1997, on UPN, https://www.imdb.com/title/tt0708953/?ref_=ttfc_fc_tt.

12. Jim McCormick, interview with author, December 19, 2018.

CHAPTER 6

1. Amy Rees Anderson, "Ubuntu—I Am Because We Are," Blog, http://www.amyreesanderson.com/blog/ubuntu-i-am -because-we-are/#.XC0dPttKipo. Accessed July 19,2019.

2. Desmond Tutu, *No Future Without Forgiveness* (New York: Image Books, 2000).

3. Clare Kelly, "How the Ubuntu Philosophy Can Have a Positive Impact on Your Business," Virgin.com, October 28, 2015,

https://www.virgin.com/virgin-unite/business-innovation
/how-ubuntu-philosophy-can-have-positive-impact-your
-business.

4. William M. Muir and David Sloan Wilson, "When the Strong Outbreed the Weak: An Interview with William Muir," The Evolution Institute, July 11, 2016, https:// evolution-institute.org/when-the-strong-outbreed-the -weak-an-interview-with-william-muir/.

5. Margaret Heffernan, "Forget the Pecking Order at Work," TEDWomen 2015, May 2015, https://www.ted.com /talks/margaret_heffernan_why_it_s_time_to_forget _the_pecking_order_at_work.

6. Heffernan, "Pecking Order."

7. Elizabeth Buchwald, "In the Wake of #MeToo, More U.S. Companies Reviewed Their Sexual Harassment Policies," *MarketWatch*, July 14, 2018, https://www.marketwatch .com/story/in-the-wake-of-metoo-more-than-half-of -companies-have-reviewed-their-sexual-harassment-policies -2018-07-10.

8. Buchwald, "In the Wake of #MeToo."

9. Gillian Tan and Katia Porzecanski, "Wall Street Rule for the #MeToo Era: Avoid Women at All Cost," *Bloomberg*, December 3, 2018, https://www.bloomberg.com/news /articles/2018-12-03/a-wall-street-rule-for-the-metoo -era-avoid-women-at-all-cost.

10. Jason Nazar quoting Wendy Lea in "35 Questions That Will Change Your Life," *Forbes*, September 5, 2013, https://www.forbes.com/sites/jasonnazar/2013/09

/05/35-questions-that-will-change-your-life/#33b
51dda5660.

11. Nazar, "35 Questions."

12. Alison Davis, "When Your CEO Won't Listen, It's Time for
You to Leave," *Inc.*, May 24, 2016, https://www.inc.com
/alison-davis/when-your-ceo-wont-listen-its-time-for-you
-to-leave.html.

13. Mike Myatt, "Why Most Leaders Need to Shut Up and
Listen," *Forbes*, February 9, 2012, https://www.forbes
.com/sites/mikemyatt/2012/02/09/why-most-leaders
-need-to-shut-up-listen/#1d93527f6ef9.

CHAPTER 7

1. Peter Block, *Stewardship*, Second Edition (San Francisco:
Berrett-Koehler Publishers, 2013), xxiv.

2. Deborah Schroeder-Saulnier, *The Power of Paradox: Harness
the Energy of Competing Ideas to Uncover Radically Innovative
Solutions* (Pompton Plains, NJ: Career Press, 2014), 24.

3. Schroeder-Saulnier, *Power of Paradox*, 24.

4. The entire exercise is explained and graphically mapped
out in "Part II: Implementing the Process," in *The Power of
Paradox* by Deborah Schroeder-Saulnier.

CHAPTER 8

1. Equilar Blog, "How Does CEO Compensation Change with
Tenure?" Equilar, August 8, 2016, https://www.equilar
.com/blogs/144-change-with-tenure.html.

2. Jeff Kauflin, "The 10 Biggest CEO Departures of 2017," *Forbes*, December 14, 2017, https://www.forbes.com/sites /jeffkauflin/2017/12/14/the-10-biggest-ceo-departures-of -2017/#5009bdb860ae.

3. Ursula Burns, "Leaders Under Pressure—Ursula Burns," *Financial Times*, YouTube video, March 11, 2018, https:// www.youtube.com/watch?v=R9Xo61vmCbY.

4. Burns, "Leaders Under Pressure."

5. Kauflin, "10 Biggest Departures."

6. Burns, "Leaders Under Pressure."

7. Burns, "Leaders Under Pressure."

8. Deborah Schroeder-Saulnier, *The Power of Paradox: Harness the Energy of Competing Ideas to Uncover Radically Innovative Solutions* (Pompton Plains, NJ: Career Press, 2014), 109.

9. Schroeder-Saulnier, *Power of Paradox*, 110.

10. Christopher (The Toy Guy) Byrne, interview with author, December 22, 2018.

11. Chris Isidore, "31,000 Toys 'R' Us Employees: No Job and No Severance," CNN Business, March 16, 2018, https:// money.cnn.com/2018/03/16/news/companies/toys-r -us-employees/index.html.

12. Malcolm Gladwell, "Malcolm Gladwell Quotes," Brainy-Quotes.com, https://www.brainyquote.com/quotes/mal-colm_gladwell_662415. Accessed July 19, 2019.

13. "Who We Are," Sisters of Notre Dame de Namur, https:// www.sndden.org/who-we-are/our-mission/. Accessed July 19, 2019.

14. Lynne Azarchi, interview with author, January 1, 2019.

15. Steven Colbert, "Doris Kearns Goodwin: What It Takes to Lead in Turbulent Times," CBS, aired on December 10, 2018, https://www.cbs.com/shows/the-late-show-with-stephen -colbert/video/xLCivx2_2KVP3hTXSMLJ3r_uqK2OOBlD /doris-kearns-goodwin-what-it-takes-to-lead-in-turbulent -times/.

CONCLUSION

1. "Self-Care Isn't Selfish—It's Essential for Our Resilience," HeartMath, https://www.heartmath.com/blog/articles/self -care-isnt-selfish-its-essential-for-our-resilience/. Accessed on July 19, 2019.

2. Meghan Rabbitt, "10 Amazing Health Benefits of Walking 30 Minutes a Day, According to Doctors" *Prevention*, June 25, 2019, https://www.prevention.com/fitness /benefits-walking-every-day.

APPENDIX A

1. Sally Percy, "What Are Donald Trump's Strengths and Weaknesses as a Leader?" *Forbes*, July 11, 2018, https://www .forbes.com/sites/sallypercy/2018/07/11/what-are -donald-trumps-strengths-and-weaknesses-as-a-leader /#49e3cbb836c7.

APPENDIX B

1. Martin Murphy, *No More Pointless Meetings* (New York: AMACOM, 2013), 9–11.

2. Murphy, *No More Meetings*,10.

3. Dean Hohn and Maryann Karinch, *Rangers Lead the Way* (Avon, MA: Adams Media, 2003), 191.

Index

About the Author

J ackie Jenkins-Scott, a Gallup Certified Strengths Coach, is a nationally recognized leader with more than three decades of experience in senior and executive leadership positions in public health and higher education. She is widely recognized as a transformational leader, helping individuals and institutions achieve high performance and strategic results. She served for twenty-one years as the President of Dimock Community Health Center and twelve years as the President of Wheelock College. In 2016, Jenkins-Scott founded JJS Advising, focusing on leadership development and organizational strategy.

Her personal commitment to improve society extends to active community and civic engagement. She is currently a member of the boards of directors of the Tufts Health Plan Foundation, the Schott Foundation for Public Education, the Center for Community Change, and the John F. Kennedy Library Foundation. For more information visit:

http://jjsadvising.com

On Twitter: @coach_leader

On Instagram: @jackie_jenkinsscott